CORRIDORS *OF* INTELLIGENCE

Revealing Politics

CORRIDORS
OF
INTELLIGENCE

Revealing Politics

DV Guruprasad (IPS)
Former
DGP : Karnataka
DG Intelligence : Karnataka

Foreword by

PM Heblikar
(Former Special Secretary : R&AW)

Manas Publications
(We Convert Fighters into Writers)
New Delhi - 110 002 (INDIA)

MANAS PUBLICATIONS
(We Convert Fighters into Writers)
(Publishers, Library Suppliers, Importers & Exporters)
4402/5-A, Ansari Road (Opp. HDFC Bank)
Darya Ganj, New Delhi - 110 002 (India)
Phones: Off.: 011-23260783, 23265523, Res.: 011-23842660
E-mail: manaspublications@gmail.com
manaspublications@yahoo.com
Website: www.manaspublications.in

ISBN 978-81-7049-555-0

₹ 795

Designed by
Veronica Grafic Arts

Printed in India at
R.K. Printers, Delhi
and published by Mrs Suman Lata for
Manas Publications
4402/5-A, Ansari Road (Opp HDFC Bank)
Darya Ganj, New Delhi - 110002 (INDIA)

Foreword

When Dr DV Guruprasad asked me to write the foreword to his book *Corridors of Intelligence: Revealing Politics,* I readily accepted it for the reason that the subject of the title itself was my bread and butter for over 38 years of my government service! It was both a sense of excitement and curiosity that prevailed on me to know of his experience in handling the arduous task of State Intelligence and delivering results to the multiple stakeholders. Intelligence is an unending game that is played 24 × 7 by its practitioners turning it into a complex and sophisticated affair.

It is common knowledge that the author embraced many facets in public life as a journalist, a career police man, an administrator of an eminent education institution as also author of many novels and publications both in Kannada and English. The book *Corridors of Intelligence: Revealing Politics,* very aptly named, is a collection of many episodes of his professional career that ranged from being a young police trainee, a probationer, a district police chief rising to top rungs of the force which saw him occupying critical posts such as Head of State Intelligence Department, State Criminal Investigation Department, Head of Training and Recruitment, and the stewardship of the Police Housing Corporation. Besides, his deputation to the Central Industrial Security Force (CISF), which gave the benefit of observing several Central Armed Police Forces and Central Police Organizations, which was to play an important role in his future.

My first meeting with him was at Delhi at the residence of a mutual friend and subsequently at Vigyan Bhavan where we were gathered for the annual conference of the Intelligence Bureau. He was then the State Intelligence chief of Karnataka. This was the setting for my introduction to Guruprasad and it grew stronger not only with each meeting but subsequently also during his stint as chief executive of the Bangalore-based Gokula Foundation.

It is seen that the Intelligence department or agencies are the often target for criticism of perceived failures especially in contemporary times. In this background, the book *Corridors of Intelligence: Revealing Politics* is a timely offering by Guruprasad on the vital role played by State Intelligence department in ensuring public safety and security at all times. He has joined several former Central Intelligence chiefs and senior officers who have written on national security by throwing light on the nature and functioning of the agencies. In India, there is considerable public shyness to discuss matters of national security in a structured manner such that a proper perspective is available. Guruprasad's book highlights internal dimensions of the subject and the multiple roles played by him during his long tenure as State Intelligence chief. He has utilized anecdotes and events in a lucid manner to deliver his message. I was particularly impressed by his deftness in navigating the political mine-fields and ensuring that the tasks before him were accomplished successfully. What is important is his equation with successive Chief Ministers of the State and other power brokers and his ability to undertake his work as per his professional instincts. He has covered this aspect in detail and this account will be worthwhile for younger generation of police officers as they will have to traverse similar routes in their career. Another important pointer that stands out is the manner of his relationship with the civilian bureaucracy in the State and also within the police force. I also relished his intuitive feelings of certain developments as also his ability to assess and analyze situations. He is candid in admitting that it is sometimes dangerous to provide political assessments. This reminded me of the hazards of dealing with such very tricky situations when in service!

There are emotions on display particularly on his missing the bus to join the Research and Analysis Wing on deputation and subsequently not making it to the elite Special Protection Group. He has articulated himself in a gracious manner on not making to the post of Head of State Police Force. There are notable references to his experience about his deployment on VVIP duties especially with the Emir of Qatar and others. The handling of several Prime Ministerial visits to the State has been mentioned in detail, which again is useful reference material for future managers of such visits. He has touched upon notable incidents in the State especially the kidnapping of Dr Rajkumar, activities of Veerappan, Naxal attacks on State police personnel and urban terrorism.

The task of a State Intelligence Chief, especially in a high profile State of Karnataka, is certainly not one of envy, it is tough, hard and unending. It relies on several professional and personal qualities, ability to creating networks across the spectrum, to be able to reasonably predict threats and challenges to public safety and security and above all ensure stability. The book attests to all above. We need to salute all those who are involved in cloak and dagger activities striving relentlessly to keep us out of harm's way. Guruprasad has done this eloquently. I congratulate him for it.

PM Heblikar
Special Secretary (Retd)
Cabinet Secretariat (R&AW)

Introduction

The civil servants and police officers, at the higher echelons in particular, are best qualified to write on the political executive and throw light on the individuals who wield power and those in the opposition who are denied power but still influence and shape the public mind. Apart from percipient journalists who care for what is abiding and not mere news breaks, it is those in the civil services who can write (though post-retirement) on the noise and chaos of our democracy which is also called the rowdiest. They can write with authority on our public life which is witnessing too much of politics and too little of democracy. Karnataka is no exception to this general rule. But what has not gone unnoticed is that very few of the State's civil servants have chosen to record their experiences. They seem to have preferred to confine their writings and thought to their notings, queries and may be misgivings to the official files.

Dr DV Guruprasad, a distinguished Indian Police Service officer, has filled a yawning gap in the contemporary political history of Karnataka by setting down the role of politicians who were in and out of power, civil servants and others in its evolution. He has not spared the growing number of courtiers, fixers and 'facilitators' who throng the corridors of power.

The best reading from Guruprasad's work is the insider account of the Chief Ministership of SM Krishna and Dharam Singh. The former enjoyed a better public image thanks to his suave ways and flamboyance, impeccable language (Kannada and English), emphasis on development and high tech industries etc. On the other hand opposite was the public perception of Dharam Singh Narayan Singh. He appeared to be homespun though worldly in his ways. The lone Rajput ruler of the State ran a coalition government pulling in different ways. His 20 months in office saw more of politics than governance. Guruprasad who was the Intelligence chief of the State police during the tenure of the two is best qualified to bring out their contrasting persona.

The one conclusion which is inevitable after reading this narrative is that over the years our chief ministers and ministers spend too much time on politics and not much on development of the State. It is no wonder few of them contribute to the advancement of the people. They are ever involved in safeguarding their *gaddis* from predators within their own parties. Few of them are willing to leave politics to the party bosses, whom they generally distrust. There is the total absence of ideology whether it is capitalism or socialism in the decisions our political leaders take. *Ad-hocism* is the rule and decisions are taken to assuage those who protest, to outwit a political opponent and most often to circumvent and ignore inconvenient judicial verdicts. Secularism is observed most in its breach with casteism and communalisms are in full play.

What is noteworthy about Dr Guruprasad's work is he narrates the events without malice towards anyone. He has placed before the people of the State an objective and truthful assessment of what has taken place.

From the narrative, it is apparent that Guruprasad enjoyed his position as the Intelligence Chief of the State. He was not a mere informer about routine developments, but at times gave unbiased opinions. Illustrative is the way he gave his assessment about the chances of the Congress party in particular elections. Though he became a 'Cassandra' for speaking the truth, the election results showed how he exposed the so-called psephologists and how the politicians had failed to assess the mood of the electorate. He is regretful that the State Intelligence failed to warn the Chief Minister of the day about the terrorists' plan to attack the Indian Institute of Science. He also mentions the embarrassment felt by the government when a Tibetan youth outwitted the might of the State and raised a black flag at the President of China who was visiting the same Indian Institute of Science.

However, Guruprasad's work is by no means an autobiography. May be he is too young to come out with a life story. Is it not said that "anecdotage is the sign of dotage". Anecdotes are corollaries of autobiographies. Apart from being a police officer who is a stickler to the laws of the land, Guruprasad is a meticulous diarist and a publicist. He has made up through his work, the lapses of most of the State's journalists in particular who have treated many an errant politician with kid gloves. Many of them including the humbugs and the corrupt got away without being exposed. Public memory is proverbially short and we need raconteurs to remind of us of even the path breaking events and developments of the recent past.

Guruprasad has had his disappointments in the IPS as for instance, not being able to serve in the RAW and denied positions due to him at the Government of India level. The truth is Karnataka is still too far away from New Delhi and even all India service officers are at a disadvantage because of that. Remember that Karnataka was one of the large States without a direct railway link to the national capital till 1978. The book makes it known to the layman that there is much more to policing than crowd control and crime detection.

Arakere Jayaram
Former Chief of Bureau
The Hindu, Bangalore

An Academician's Opinion

When you compile scenes from real life you have an anecdotal autobiography, one that is infinitely more interesting than the standard biography which blandly lays out facts, names, dates and generalities about events. That is how I see Dr DV Guruprasad's book *Corridors of Intelligence: Revealing Politics.*

True to its name this book is about the vivid intrigue and action involving the 'assignments' of a secret agent and espionage. Equally, or perhaps more, interesting is that the book explores events leading to several twists and turns in Karnataka politics that have had a bearing on the policy-making and the political lives in Karnataka.

The events covered in the book go back to the period of Devaraj Urs eventually reaching up to Yeddyurappa's regime. This is a long time in the political life of a State and the book encompasses it passionately. Although I do not see any specific intention or justification on the part of the author for publishing this book it is reason enough that such experiences have been shared and that exposure has been gained among politically elite circles.

Incidentally these interactions, at the time of writing this book, seem to have unleashed a series of behavioural patterns of the political and higher bureaucracy as the author watched them unravelling, exposing their day-to-day dilemma and the common concerns they have as ordinary human beings. In the whole of this narrative the author seems to be an anchor divulging key information which otherwise might never have reached the ears of either the ordinary public or those specialized in the study of politics. There are several incidents like the Banamathi black magic, the Datta Jayanti issue, issues concerning Naxalism, democratic number games and how they play up in politics, the idea of losing to win etc, which call the attention of the reader - thanks to their exclusivity and significance in understanding Indian politics in general and, especially, the value-laden politics in Karnataka.

The book is divided into 18 chapters and as the Preface lets you in with curiosity the contents of these chapters carries the reader with eagerness to explore more and more to unravel the political and social events side by side. The beauty of the writing lies in the author's skill to orchestrate his personal interest (autobiographical) with his experience as a police officer (on the job) and present them in a lucid manner within the political space and time without breaching the trust of his professional commitments.

In that sense this work is a political almanac which focuses on narrating the events as they unfolded without being coloured wildly by authors' pen. This is a good thing; it is also a rare sight to behold these days. From the Preface itself he clears to the reader that he simply wishes to share some interesting experiences of his through this book and carefully travels through the events that he was a witness to. His sharing of these events he witnessed using adjectives sparingly and offering explanations using few expressions without showing his emotions about the systemic contours too vividly makes space for the reader to construe many facts between the lines. For instance, an expression like "... instead of concentrating on the officials at the lowest rung, as it was the earlier practice, the Bureau targeted senior officials ..." cleverly explains the nature of the governments then and of the rulers.

As an author he uses appropriately this space to share his personal achievements, explaining through them the nature of governance, politics and his reverence to capable officers and astute politicians. This indeed is the hall mark of the author throughout book.

Given the political turmoil of the 1970s and '80s and his travel through the passage of three decades till 2010-11 witnessing the unfolding of the political drama as an eyewitness - to the rise and fall of the regional satraps, the wicked ways of politics and the cunningness of 'Self' prevailing over public interests and most of all capturing them through his pen and vocabulary to reconstruct the events for a reader is indeed a rare craft worthy of admiration without bias. These narratives not only exhibit the authors' closeness to political leadership in his official capacity but also enhance the authenticity of the book allowing the reader to perceive the events as they outspread. There are many such events that the author explains in this book that is not available to readers in the open. For example we get great insights into the personalities of and events that involve Devaraj Urs, Gundu Rao or Kaarthikeyan and many others who matter. For a reviewer it's a feast as also for an aficionado of politics. However, it is impossible to allude to them all in a review as one can understand.

From the first chapter to the last, Dr Guruprasad unfolds a lot of action in each chapter keeping his grip on his writing and on the reader's interest. Most interesting for me among these were his recollections of the stamp paper scam, the dramatic changes in the State's political scenario, the arrest of Uma Bharti, and the Naxal problem taking centerstage, the growing tensions within the Congress party and his excellent chapter aptly titled "Beyond Intelligence Work".

In many chapters the author writes about the political events as they unfolded and leaves it to the reader to make further judgments; Gundu Rao's election in Somwarpet and Mrs Gandhi's visit to Bellary where a brick was hurled at her car is in focus. While explaining these political events the author successfully brings in the trials and tribulations of the police with his personal anecdotes. These in a way throw light on the inter- and intra-relationships between various political, bureaucratic and policing institutions.

The penning of his memoir in an artistic vogue exposing the nuances of his (police life) hard life in places like Delhi and yet being positive in all odd situations is the strength of the author's will and writing. In the immediate instance post the Bidar Blast, his writing on the 'Adamant VP Singh' and the 'Sportive Rajiv Gandhi' are subheadings that are suggestive of his ability to grasp issues and personalities. Similarly many of the titles and subtitles in the chapters are clearly suggestive of his views as an author and he seems to have his own reason for that. For example his title "Dramatic Changes in the State's Political Scenario" is truly dramatic and only when one reads the chapter will one come to know of it - but it does not stop the reader to have a differing point of view. Here some of the conversations between Shivakumar and Krishna, the then CM, are open to the world for the first time from the author's pen. For a serious political analyst and a political scientist, or otherwise for those interested in politics, these facts throw open umpteen ways of looking at the events that have stretched then and, significantly enough, throws light on the importance of intelligence input and the ordinary ways of helplessness of a decision-maker even at the helm of affairs.

"Growing Tensions Within the Congress Party" is yet another piece of writing where personalized conversations are out in the public domain. In this case it is Dharam Singh who confides with this police officer his feelings. The beauty of these lie in the explorations of various dimensions of personalities throughout the book; sometimes it is a bureaucrat and sometimes a political leader when in the midst of all this is the author exploring a lot of social and intra-personal relationships through his writing.

It is true that as a reviewer I cannot go on writing about every chapter but I can definitely bring out the finality with which the author has penned the many politico-social events as a bystander and, at times, as a player. What holds me as a reader is his ability to not only explain the political events even as an outsider but also carry his perceptions graphically in time to record them for the reader. I rarely see the author participate in these events even in his writing but he sincerely attempts to explain the events threadbare to hold the readers fixed to his narrations.

There are too many actors in this book. Some have a small role to play while others have larger, more important ones. Yet the author has not etched any character here beyond their real time frame. Thus this book emphasizes events and characters in equal footing transcending and setting itself apart from the ordinary collection of anecdotal pieces.

The book is contemporary in its content as the events described in it are merely a three decades or so old. Perhaps the book should have been released earlier for people to read with even greater interest; nevertheless it will help understand the politics - the inside stories - for many who teach Karnataka Politics as a paper at universities. This book is a must for all universities and research centres where politics is taught professionally.

Lastly, is the book without limitations? It is true that there are limitations. Many of these memoirs though written by professionals in a particular field will be limited in their expressions to dramatise the events to make the reading fascinating or enthralling. This book too in that sense needs the touch of professionals. One may argue that it is not the intention, but the language correction in that direction is a need. Nobody is telling that the facts must be twisted - but we must try and make it absorbing. Further there are some abrupt endings to many events presented in the book. In case of Dr Rajkumar's abduction there were news of a large chunk of money exchanging hands, the involvement of LTTE etc, however there are not many facts covered relating to these which are of interest generally. There are some contradictions too. Like SM Krishna not being outwardly religious - this is contrary to the belief that SMK was quite religious. There are many areas it is felt that an intelligence officer could have stretched beyond recounting of events and elucidated to the reader the truth about the events helping him to reach the bottom of the truth. Beyond outlining of characters by giving more facts and figures - the author could have dug in to the truth about the Naxalite attacks or about Saket Rajan, stamp paper scam etc, avoiding additional explanations in some cases to make the reading somewhat exciting.

Having said these I must record my sincere appreciation for the efforts of the officer to have given us this window to understand the stark realities of politics, political class and the events that surrounds it. In a country where such memoirs are yet to become the new normal despite the right regime - this book is a ray of hope emanating from the cupboards of memory of a competent officer is worth a reading. As the title suggests the book undoubtedly unveils the "Cloak and a Dagger Affair" in Indian politics in brief and in Karnataka politics in particular. I wish him the best and hope that he would write more and more boldly in the years to come.

Dr Harish Ramaswamy
Professor of Political Science
Director, UGC-HRDC
Karnatak University
Dharwad

Preface

As an IPS officer, I had the good fortune of seeing many influential, important and famous political figures at very close quarters. Thanks to my association with VIP Security work, I could keenly observe the personality traits of many of them and discern their special qualities as individuals.

I learnt a lot from observing people in power. Contrary to the popular belief, most politicians are very intelligent and know the pulse of people. They remain close to their voters and know what exactly is happening in their constituencies. They keep their eyes and ears to the ground constantly getting information from multiple sources. If they were not street smart people, they wouldn't be where they were.

As the Head of the Intelligence Wing of Karnataka Police for three years, and as Superintendent in the same wing for a year, I worked with four Chief Ministers with whom I interacted on a daily basis. I was witness to many important events that shaped the history of Karnataka. I was in a position to know the how and why of so many incidents that impacted the citizens of the State. Later, as the Head of CID (Crime), I once again worked closely with the Chief Minister of Karnataka. I supervised the investigation of 'sensational' cases of those days as the DGP, CID.

While heading the Karnataka Information Department, I had the opportunity of observing closely those not in politics like artists, journalists, film personalities and other creative people.

After my retirement from the IPS in 2011, I thought that I should share some interesting details about my experience of closely working with, not one but four Chief Ministers. I wanted to share with the readers the various personal characteristics of the Chief Ministers, with whom I worked and portray the lesser known aspects of their personality. I wanted to narrate the background of how important events shaped in Karnataka those days.

It was easy for me to write this book since maintaining a diary had been my habit since my younger days. While I have heavily relied on my diary entries, I have taken care to narrate events in as objective and as truthful a manner as possible. The narration is mainly based on my personal recollections of events. They are not word-for-word transcripts as while writing my diary, I recorded the day's events from memory. I have narrated the events in such a way that they evoke the feelings and meaning of what was said at the given instance. While narrating the incidents, if I have caused anyone any pain or embarrassment it is purely unintentional. I crave their indulgence.

Though this book is not my autobiography as its focus is on the Chief Ministers of Karnataka, I could not but help write about myself in order to make the reader get the proper perspective. There are definitely autobiographical elements for the sake of reference. I think they are inevitable. I have also mentioned some interesting anecdotes to break the monotony.

This book attempts to trace the political history of Karnataka between the years 2003 and 2006.

I am grateful to my sister Nandini Kapdi, journalists Asha Krishnaswamy and Arakere Jayaram for going through the manuscript and helping me in making it more readable. I am indebted to my friend Pratap Heblikar, Former Special Secretary, Cabinet Secretariat for writing the Foreword to this book. I am also grateful to Arakere Jairam, Former Bureau Chief of *The Hindu* for writing the introduction.

SK Das, former Secretary to the Government of India (Department of Space and Department of Atomic Energy) and T Madiyal, the former DG and IGP of Karnataka, graciously went through the manuscript and gave their valuable suggestions. I am indebted to both of them.

I am indeed thankful to Prof Harish Ramaswamy for reviewing the manuscript and pen his critical opinion on my work.

I am indebted to Vivek Garg, Adviser, Manas Publications, New Delhi for arranging to get this book published. In fact this is the third book of mine which the publisher has ventured to bring out.

My family members have always been my readers and my bitterest critics. I am grateful to my wife Swarna and children Sumukh and Apoorva.

DV Guruprasad (IPS)

Notes:

1. I have not used the new names of places in Karnataka like Bengaluru, Shivamogga, Ballari etc and have stuck to the older names.
2. I have not used honorifics for any person out of convenience and not out of disrespect.

DISCLAIMER

I have taken care to narrate events in this book objectively and truthfully. The narration is based on my recollection of events. They are not word-for-word transcripts. I have retold them in a way that evokes the feelings and meaning of what was said at the given instance. It is not my intention to cause pain or hurt, or to denigrate, or to lower any living or dead person's image in society. If in recording the events, I have unwittingly caused anyone any embarrassment, or hurt or pain, I seek their forgiveness.

AUTHOR

Contents

1

My Foray into Police Service

Fed on a diet of spy thrillers since my school days, especially the novels of Ian Fleming, I had an innate desire for working in the Intelligence organisations of the country, like the Intelligence Bureau, or the Research and Analysis Wing (R&AW). I was aware that officers in Intelligence work as eyes and ears of the government and hence have access to people in power and have a role in shaping events that affect the lives of many. I had also been told that if lucky one could live in foreign countries.

I got selected for the Indian Police Service in the year 1976. By then I was 25 years old and had obtained a post-graduate degree in English literature. My ranking in the examinations was quite high and I was hopeful of getting my home cadre of Karnataka. As every IPS officer had to work for some years with the Government of India on deputation, I hoped to get deputed to one of the Central Intelligence agencies when I got promoted to the rank of Superintendent of Police. Those days, the Intelligence Bureau had a scheme called 'earmarking scheme' through which those officers who had a higher rank in the entrance examination were picked by the Bureau and trained to become Intelligence Officers. Several officers from Karnataka had gone away on deputation very early in their careers and I hoped to be like them.

While undergoing my foundation training course in Mussoorie, my batch mate in the IPS, Alok Joshi (who later became the Head of the country's external Intelligence agency R&AW and also the Chairman of National Technical Research

Organisation, NTRO) introduced me to an uncle of his who was at that time working in the R&AW. Though the senior Joshi was not an IPS officer, he had been selected by the R&AW for a middle-level post on deputation. Through diligence and hard work he had risen to the rank of SP and had been posted in a foreign country and had come to Delhi on a holiday. After spending half a day with him, I had decided to join the R&AW, the moment I became eligible for Central deputation.

I knew that to realize my dream, I had to complete my institutional training in the National Police Academy, and practical training in the State to which I would be allotted for service. I was told that normally after completion of four years of service, including the training period, an IPS officer would be promoted to the rank of Superintendent of Police. I had to therefore, wait for at least four more years to even try for Central deputation.

While undergoing training in the National Police Academy, I was allotted to my home State of Karnataka. My parents were quite happy to learn this. After completing my training at NPA, I reported to the Police Chief in Bangalore, Albert Manoraj. I was posted to Gulbarga district for my practical training after undergoing ten-week familiarization training in Mysore.

During my training in Gulbarga in the year 1978, the election to the State Legislative Assembly had been announced and I was lucky to be part of the election process and get first-hand knowledge about various facets connected with elections so early in my career. Immaterial of one's liking or dislike for politics, IPS officers have to be abreast with political developments as they closely work with men in power. Though I had no special interest in politics as such, my work demanded me to be a keen observer of political developments which I did. This became useful to me in my later career in Intelligence.

I vividly remember doing *bandobust* duties for the election meetings in the district as well as the function organized to felicitate the newly elected MLAs, which included Mallikarjuna Kharge and Dharam Singh from the Congress, who later came to occupy important positions in the State. In the 1978 Legislative Assembly elections, the Congress party which won 149 seats formed the government. Devaraj Urs was re-elected as the CM for a second term.

Some political events of that period need mention here to give a better perspective on the narrative I am presenting. After Indira Gandhi had lost the 1977 parliamentary elections, her party had decided that she should enter Parliament through the bye-election route. DB Chandre Gowda, the MP from Chikmagalur in Karnataka decided to vacate his seat to facilitate her election. The bye-election were held in November 1978. To manage this election, which had gained international attention, HT Sangliana, who was the SP, Gulbarga and under whom I was being trained as an IPS probationer, had been transferred to Chikmagalur as SP.

In the bye-election, Mrs Gandhi defeated her nearest rival Veerendra Patil (a native of Gulbarga district and a former Karnataka Chief Minister) of the Janata Party and returned to Parliament.

The Chikmagalur bye-election became a pointer to the forthcoming changes in the political climate of the country. At the Centre, cracks had developed in the coalition partnership leading to the resignation of Prime Minister Morarji Desai. Charan Singh formed the government with the support of the Congress but he too had to resign within six months of assumption of office when the Congress party withdrew support to the government. This necessitated fresh elections to Parliament in the early 1980.

Meanwhile, all was not well with the Congress party too. In July 1979, the party had split for the second time and the then Chief Minister of Karnataka, Devaraj Urs became the leader of a faction of the party called Indian National Congress (Urs). The faction showing allegiance to Indira Gandhi came to be known as the Indian National Congress (Indira).

When the elections to Parliament were held in 1980, of the 28 Parliamentary seats in Karnataka, the INC (Indira) won a whopping 27 seats. From the Gulbarga Parliamentary constituency, the INC(I) had given the ticket to Dharam Singh who had been earlier elected in 1978 as MLA from the Jewargi assembly constituency. He won the election. The spectacular victory of candidates from the INC(I) in the elections and the decimation of the fledgling Congress (Urs) party resulted in the collapse of Devaraj Urs government in Karnataka in January 1980. R Gundu Rao succeeded him as the CM.

In those years the entire Hyderabad-Karnataka area was quite underdeveloped. Looking back, I feel amused at the way we made phone calls those days. There was no direct dialling facility. We had to book a call through a telephone operator. To make a call to Bangalore, we had to book a 'trunk call' and sit in front of the phone for hours together waiting for the calls to materialize. We had to book 'lightening calls' if the matter was urgent. Those days we, in the police department, entirely depended on the police wireless system for our communications.

Fortunately, things changed for the better when CM Stephen was elected to the Lok Sabha from Gulbarga Parliamentary constituency. Exactly as Chandre Gowda had made way for Indira Gandhi in 1978, Dharam Singh, who had won the Gulbarga Lok Sabha seat in the 1980 elections, resigned his Parliamentary seat even before taking the oath of office and helped CM Stephen become the Union Communications Minister. Soon afterward, Gulbarga got a modern electronic telephone exchange which became the envy of bigger cities. At the time of canvassing for the elections, Stephen was introduced to the voters as 'Tippanna' so that they would think the 'Keralite' candidate to be their own.

During the split in the Congress party, Dharam Singh had remained loyal to Indira Gandhi. He was one of the first persons invited by Gundu Rao to join the Karnataka cabinet as he continued to represent the Jewargi assembly constituency, which he had won in 1978 and which he had not resigned to contest the Lok Sabha elections.

On successful completion of my practical training in Gulbarga district, I was posted in November 1978 as Assistant Superintendent of Police of Hospet in Bellary district. The Sub-Division consisted of only two talukas, Hospet and Sandur. While Sandur, with its iron ore and manganese mines, gave rise to frequent labour related problems, the richly irrigated taluka of Hospet was largely peaceful with periodic demands from sugarcane growers for higher prices for their produce. With the World Heritage site Hampi nearby, Hospet was thronged by tourists, many of them hippies, causing its own problems for police. Mining those days was limited to a few mines and was not being done on a large scale. The demand for the ore by China prior to the Olympic Games in Beijing in 2008 was the cause for the sudden spurt in mining activity later on. The Vijayanagar Steel Plant at Tornagallu had not even been set up then and only a foundation stone laid by the PM Mrs Gandhi was in existence.

I had a very thrilling and satisfactory tenure as ASP of Hospet. The busting of an international racket of idol smugglers was the highlight of my tenure.

During that period SA Subaiah, a 1968 batch IPS officer of Karnataka cadre, was working as the Assistant Director of R&AW in Bangalore. In connection with tracking a Pakistani citizen who had come to Hospet, he came to my office and we had a long chat about my possible induction into the organization. He suggested that I should work as a district SP for a few years and then join R&AW. He had suggested that if I wanted I could resign from the IPS after going on deputation to the organization and permanently work with the R&AW. He named several IPS officers who had done so. Hence, I decided to wait for some more time to realize my dream. In June 1980, I was promoted to the rank of SP and posted to Bidar district.

Soon after my promotion, I began my efforts to go on deputation to R&AW, but my father, who was a government officer then, was against me going on deputation so soon in my career. I was his only son and he didn't want me to work either in Delhi or in distant foreign lands. He had a friend, an IAS officer who was working in the Ministry of Home Affairs then and through his help thwarted my effort to go on deputation to R&AW. Though thoroughly disappointed, I decided to bide for my time.

'Bhanamati'

While working in Bidar, I came across a strange phenomenon called 'Bhanamati', which was a type of black magic. Those persons who wished to wreck vengeance on their opponents would hire a sorcerer, with whose help would cause various types of harm to the victim and his family. The harm would come in the form of sudden and unexplained shower of stones on the victim's house, spoiling of the food kept on the stove for cooking, tearing of clothes kept for drying on the clothesline, sudden physical afflictions to the victim which would appear like epileptic attacks, important objects suddenly catching fire etc. Though some bodily harm would be caused, it would not result in death or serious injury.

I was of the opinion that 'Bhanamati' was nothing but a type of black magic. Hence I expressed my shock at the registration of complaints in the police stations against those suspected of committing 'Bhanamati'. My officers politely told me that I should not comment on a phenomenon that I didn't understand. They informed me that in the erstwhile Hyderabad State, the police establishment consisted of a 'Bhanamati Squad' headed by an Inspector of Police which would investigate all such complaints. Some retired police officers told me that the technique of 'Bhanamati' originated in China and came to India via Bhutan and that one should not brush it off and it was the duty of the police to help citizens in distress.

On visiting the houses of victims who had lodged complaints of 'Bhanamati', I had noted that the victims were mostly from the economically and socially backward classes and generally uneducated. On speaking to the victims, I had felt that most of them were imagining situations or were exaggerating certain events which they could not understand or those which could not be easily explained.

Complaints of 'Bhanamati' were being registered in police stations under the head of mischief, arson as contemplated in the Indian Penal Code as no other law had been enacted to deal with such cases. I had also noticed that most of these complaints had been closed as undetected since the person who practised Bhanamati would never come out in the open.

Since the police were unable to arrest any practitioner of 'Bhanamati' the usual practice in the villages of the district was to physically attack anyone who was suspected to practice 'Bhanamati'. A good number of such suspects had been brutally attacked and sometimes lynched by enraged villagers and hence the complaints of 'Bhanamati' could not be taken lightly.

To examine and report about the phenomenon of 'Bhanamati' in the districts of Hyderabad-Karnataka area, the government headed by Chief Minister Gundu Rao, appointed a committee under the chairmanship of Dr H Narasimhaiah, the Vice-Chancellor of Bangalore University, and a known rationalist. I also appeared before this committee and gave my views when it visited Bidar. Incidentally, Dr H Narasimhaiah was my teacher and mentor and he was happy to see me as SP of a district.

The committee later submitted a report stating that there was no scientific basis for 'Bhanamati'.

Caste Conflict and Transfer

A serious caste conflict between Lingayats and Scheduled Castes occurred in Bidar district in April 1981 resulting in heavy loss of lives and property. Probably thinking that the district administration had not handled the situation effectively, both the District Magistrate and I were transferred out of the district in May 1981. For me, it was a premature transfer as I had not even completed a year's tenure in the district.

I was posted as Superintendent of Police in the State anti-corruption branch. Those days the anti-corruption branch was known as State Vigilance Commission and was headed by a retired High Court Judge, RG Desai. C Dinakar was the DIG of the Bureau of Investigation and to assist him there were half a dozen Superintendents of Police. Kasturi Rangan and I were the SPs working in Bangalore. At that time, the wing had become very active and had successfully prosecuted many senior and influential public servants. Some of them were the then Secretary of the Public Works Department, and the then Health Secretary. Instead of concentrating on officials at the lower rung, as was the earlier practice, the Bureau targeted senior officials from the Public Works, Irrigation and Transport departments. Some IAS and IPS officers also came under our scanner.

I cannot forget the search conducted on a senior officer of the PWD who claimed proximity to the then Chief Minister Gundu Rao. During the search of his house, he claimed that after the recent bereavement of the CM, he had organized the religious rites connected with the death and showed me some documents to prove it. He claimed that he had got a thousand copies of *Bhagavad Geeta* printed and distributed to the people who attended the '13th-day Vaikunta Samaradhana' function. He also showed us photographs of himself with Gundu Rao. We were unmoved by his claims and went ahead with our search.

During the search we found a document indicating that he had a locker in a bank in Bangalore. We decided to go to the bank and search it the next day. I was given this task and I asked him to come to the bank with the locker key. When we met in the bank, he told us that he had lost the locker key. I didn't know what to do. I consulted my higher-ups and on their advice decided to get the locker broken open. The bank officers were perplexed by this request as it was the first time such a request had been made. When convinced, they tried to get the manufacturer of the locker to help us. The locker of the officer was broke open using a welding torch. When opened, I found bundles of currency notes inside the locker apart from some documents. It took us hours counting the currency notes. As I completed writing the seizure memo and asked the officer to sign it, he took me aside and offered me 50% of the notes if I let him off the hook!

Later on, we filed the chargesheet in the case, and after a protracted trial, I was told that he had escaped conviction. After two years or so, I happened to meet him on a busy street in Bangalore and he proudly told me that we couldn't do much to him!

As an active member of the Bureau of Investigation, I too gained sufficient 'notoriety' for successfully conducting 'raids' (searches of office and residential premises of the 'tainted' officers). I had also succeeded in getting a number of big fish into the anti-corruption net. Desai was quite pleased with my work and encouraged me to conduct more and more 'raids'.

Within six months of my joining the Vigilance Commission, I learnt that some senior public servants for whom we had become a thorn in the flesh were pressurizing the government to get us transferred. Being the youngest and junior-most officer in the Bureau of Investigation then, I became the first target. Soon I was transferred and posted as SP of Hassan district. Desai refused to relieve me from the Vigilance Commission and succeeded in getting my transfer orders cancelled. This was in early 1982.

A few weeks later, in April 1982, when Desai summoned me to his office and told me that I was being relieved to join the State Intelligence Wing, I was pleasantly surprised. He told me that he had been invited by Chief Minister Gundu Rao for a breakfast meeting that morning and during this meeting, the CM had desired my posting to the State Intelligence which was directly functioning under him. Desai had reluctantly agreed to the request of the CM. I felt very happy that at last my desire of working in the Intelligence Wing was being fulfilled.

I was acquainted with Gundu Rao, as he was quite friendly with film personalities and my brother-in-law 'Edakallu Gudda' Chandrasekhar happened to be a Kannada film actor. I had met him in 1979 when he had come to Hospet along with the other leaders of the Congress(I) like Bangarappa. When I was working as SP of Bidar district in 1980, I had been given the task of translating the CM's English speech into Kannada in a public function. He was pleased with my translation and had told me that he had heard about me through Chandrasekhar.

On getting relief from the State Vigilance Commission, I reported to DR Kaarthikeyan, the DIG and Chief of State Intelligence. At that time he was considered the 'most influential and powerful' police officer in Karnataka. He was to later adorn many important assignments. He headed the Special Investigation Team that probed the assassination of Rajiv Gandhi by LTTE apart from heading the Central Bureau of Investigation. When I met him he told me that he wanted me to work as his Staff Officer, which I felt was a great honour. A staff officer is expected to assist the Head of the institution in all official matters including file work. I was also asked to look after Bangalore Rural Division. Several eminent IPS officers were already working in the Intelligence Wing and I was very happy that my former boss in Bellary, KR Srinivasan would be my colleague. He was the SP in-charge of Administration.

In the first few weeks, I found my work to be of a routine nature and unexciting. I was asked to read all the daily papers, mark important news items and prepare a gist of subjects which had caught the attention of the media. I was to concentrate on news stories which were critical of the government. I was also told to go through the situation reports received from our field staff as well as the District Superintendents of Police and prepare a report.

As I had started my career as a reporter-cum-sub-editor of a newspaper, I enjoyed doing this job. I was reading at least twenty newspapers daily. Since I didn't know Tamil, Malayalam and Urdu languages certain police officers who knew these languages would help me know what was reported in those papers. In those days, there were no television channels and we had to depend on print media, and All India Radio to know what was happening around us.

Intelligence gathering essentially involves gauging the mood of the people and assessing what is likely to happen in the future. It is an intelligent analysis of an array of information. In the police department, Intelligence is collected for the purpose of crime prevention, crime detection and also maintenance of law and order. While Intelligence relating to crime is collected by a unit called Crime Branch, Intelligence not related to crime, but mostly related to public order is collected by the Special Branch. Every district has a Special Branch to do this work. Officers working in both the branches do not wear their uniform and move around towns and villages and gather nuggets of information which are of importance for the prevention of crime and maintenance of law and order.

The State Intelligence Wing is an establishment separate from the district and city police set-up. It works independently and has its own branches in virtually every district. It is sanctioned a large manpower for Intelligence and security duties. Apart from utilizing the Intelligence collected by the personnel working in the district/city special branches, the State Intelligence Wing also makes use of 'sources' who may comprise of ordinary citizens, political personages, media personnel and anyone who has and who can part with useful information. Since information does not come free, the sources have to paid/rewarded.

Intelligence is collected in two ways - through Human beings (HUMINT) and by use of technical gadgets (TECHINT). The Intelligence agencies also use various technical gadgets to track the movements of individuals and to eavesdrop on their conversations and monitor their internet usage. Collection of Intelligence through technical gadgets was not as easy as it is today because the Internet and cell phones were used rarely.

We would request the authorities to permit tapping of the target individuals' landlines and to intercept their postal communications.

Many governments have used and still use the Intelligence Wing of the police department to learn about political developments. Assessment of poll prospects is one such.

Nowadays there are hundreds of agencies who are involved in assessing the mood of the electorate and predicting election results. There are qualified psephologists to do such work. Surveys are conducted before polls and also when a voter has actually cast his vote and survey results are predicted. Thirty-five years ago, no such facilities were available to the political masters and the ruling political party invariably depended on the police Intelligence Wing for knowing the voter's mind.

Within a few weeks of my joining State Intelligence, bye-election to the Assembly Constituency of Bidar was announced consequent to the demise of the sitting MLA Veerasetty Kushnoor. As I had worked in that district only a few months earlier, I was asked to proceed there and make an assessment of the political situation in the constituency. I made three trips to Bidar in May 1982.

Though the work of assessing the prospects of the ruling party in the bye-election was quite new to me, since I had made a number of friends in Bidar, despite my short stint as SP there, I was able to gather that the Congress party had an edge. During one of my trips to Bidar, I was flying to Hyderabad from Bangalore. As I boarded the plane, I saw the former CM of Karnataka Devaraj Urs sitting in the front row. As the plane took off, I went towards Urs and introduced myself. He asked me to sit beside him in the vacant seat next to him. As we started chatting, I told him that I was going to Bidar for election assessment and steered our discussion towards the elections. He gave me a lot of insights and as the plane was landing he told me, "Tell Gundu Rao that his candidate would win the elections," and shook hands with me.

Knowing that he had lost his power when the Congress party split, and that I was working with Gundu Rao, I was amazed at his grace in giving me so much of political information. In my assessment too I mentioned that Mohsin Kamal, the Congress candidate would win. And he won by a margin of over 4,000 votes defeating his nearest BJP rival Narayana Rao Manhalli.

When I hit the bull's eye with my assessment, my stature rose in the department though I was the junior most SP working there. More important tasks started coming to my desk. The task of preparing the Daily Situation Report meant for the Chief Minister and top officials of the government was entrusted to me and due to which I had to work for long hours in the office. Kaarthikeyan was a hard taskmaster and being a workaholic, he expected officers working with him to follow suit. My wife used to be very unhappy that even in a non-uniformed job, I had to work for such long hours and not devote even an hour for my son who was only one year old. All the officers of SP level had to work by turns even on Sundays and holidays.

When the 7th Non-Aligned Summit was hosted in Delhi in March 1983, I was one of the five SP rank officers from Karnataka sent to take care of the massive security duties. The others were Subhash Bharani, T Harikrishna, and T Jayaprakash. T Jayaprakash later worked as IG, Intelligence and my second in command when I headed the State Intelligence Wing. Harikrishna was to lay his life later in the police fight against the forest brigand Veerappan.

Security Liaison for the Emir of Qatar

The Central Intelligence Bureau trained us for almost two months in its training school in Delhi and this training became very valuable to me in my later career. I was assigned to be the Security Liaison Officer to the Emir of Qatar. Those days Qatar was not as rich and famous as it is now. I had to literally struggle to get to know more about that country and its ruler

HE Khalifa Bin Hamad Al Thani. Since there was no internet facility then, I had to depend on *Manorama Year Book* and such other reference material.

All the heads of State/government were accommodated in five-star hotels along with their entourage and we were also to stay with them. Each dignitary was provided with a Mercedes Benz limousine, and a pilot and escort vehicle. My duty was to travel with the dignitary in his car and liaise with the Delhi Police and other security agencies during the VIP movements and follow the routes and instructions given by the Control Room. The officers in the pilot and escort vehicles were from Delhi Police and Central Paramilitary Forces and were to function under my command.

On the designated day, the Emir arrived at Palam airport in his special plane. A new building had been constructed at the airport only to receive and see off the heads of State/ government attending the NAM. This building has now become Terminal Two of Indira Gandhi International Airport.

When we, the designated Security Officers, had been taken to this building a few days prior to NAM for familiarization, I had seen Indira Gandhi supervising various arrangements. Smt Pupul Jayakar, who was known as 'Culture Czarina' was with her and Mrs Gandhi was giving directions about the placement of various paintings in the hall. We had overheard her telling the officials to remove a particular type of curtain. I was amazed that the Prime Minister of India was so personally involved in giving the world leaders a good picture of our country.

A few minutes before the Emir landed, another plane brought his personal car. His security chief who had come to Delhi in advance met me and told me that the Emir wanted to travel in his own car which had come a few minutes earlier and not use the one provided by the Indian government. I put my foot down and told him that the Emir had to travel only in the car provided by our government due to security concerns. He was disappointed. After the Emir was formally received by a

Union Minister, I took him to the Oberoi Hotel, where he was scheduled to stay. During the journey to the hotel, he lit a cigarette and offered one to me. I politely refused. I guessed that though he knew English fairly well, he did not wish to make it apparent.

The next day, I accompanied the Emir to the opening function of NAM and was excited to see the legendary Fidel Castro along with Prime Minister Indira Gandhi. What surprised me was that the Secretary-General of NAM Natwar Singh didn't recognize the VIP whom I had accompanied and I had to whisper in his ears that the VIP I had accompanied was the Emir of Qatar. The Emir didn't sit through the entire deliberations and returned to the hotel after about an hour and a half.

While at the hotel I was informed by the Emir's Security Chief that Palestine Liberation Organisation Chief Yasser Arafat would be visiting the Emir in his suite in the hotel. I was quite nervous because the threat perception to Arafat was very high. I remembered the classes in which we were taught how to tackle security threats and see that the visiting dignitaries are not harmed.

I went to the hotel lobby to receive Arafat. The puny leader came surrounded by his special bodyguards and when we led him to the elevator to take him to the sixth-floor room of the Emir, Arafat simply shook his head and started climbing the stairs, two at a time.

He ran up all the six floors of the staircase so fast that when I caught up with him, I was panting. I led him to the Emir and waited in the ante-chamber. He was closeted with the Emir for almost an hour. I learnt later that the PLO leader had come seeking financial assistance.

The Emir preferred to stay in the hotel rather than attend deliberations in Vigyan Bhavan and hence I didn't have much work. One evening he went to his Embassy where a dinner in his honour had been organized. There was a lot of wining and dining and merriment in the party.

The next day, the Emir decided to leave for Doha and before leaving the hotel, he called me and offered me an envelope and thanked me. When I returned to my room and opened it, I found ten crisp US $ 100 bills inside. I immediately went to the Security Officer of the Emir and returned the envelope. Telling me that returning a gift by the Emir amounts to disrespect, he took me to the Emir. I explained to the Emir that as per the Conduct Rules for All India Service officers, I could not accept expensive or cash gifts. I told him that I would be most happy to receive a signed photograph of him. He was perplexed and didn't know what to do. He invited me to visit his country and be his guest which I gladly accepted. (When I did visit Qatar many years later, I found the soft-spoken Emir had been deposed by his son and that he was living in exile.)

The security duties for NAM made me learn a lot of things related to VIP Security. I cannot forget the party hosted to us by Prime Minister Indira Gandhi after the successful completion of the meet. She came to each and every one of us and made us feel comfortable and thanked us.

I had experienced the hospitality of Mrs Gandhi even earlier. When I was working as Assistant Superintendent of Police in Hospet, she had visited Hampi in 1979 to meet the senior pontiff of Kanchi Kamakoti Math His Holiness Chandrasekhara Saraswati Swamiji who was camping there. We had prepared a helipad close to the cave in which Swamiji was staying. We had been told that her meeting was a personal one and no one, including security staff, should be allowed to be near her. On the day of her visit, Swamiji was observing silence and Swamiji had replied to her questions in sign language. After the one-on-one meeting, she drove to Hospet where the local legislator Narayana Swamy had organized a lunch for her at his residence.

As part of her security team I was with her, but since I had not been invited for lunch I was waiting outside the hall where Mrs Gandhi had sat for lunch. She had seen me and other police officers standing outside and asked Narayana Swamy to invite us for lunch. We were made to sit on a table opposite hers and she made us feel very comfortable.

During that visit of the ex-PM to Hampi and Hospet, what had surprised me was that the then Chief Minister Devaraj Urs had not come to Hampi to personally receive her. He had deputed Sadyojatha, Cabinet Minister representing Bellary district, to receive Mrs Gandhi at Hampi. When within a few weeks of her visit to Hampi, the Indian National Congress split with Devaraj Urs becoming the leader of INC (Urs), things became clearer to me. I also guessed that she must have come to seek the blessings of the Swamiji for the eventful political decisions she was soon to take.

Looking back at Indira Gandhi's concern towards the security personnel, I felt that it was the irony of fate that at a later date her own trusted security guards had assassinated her mercilessly.

2

Elections to the Legislature Assembly in 1983 and Thereafter

On my return to Bangalore, events unfolded very fast. The elections to the State Legislative Assembly were slated to be held in the next few months and we were asked to prepare for it. I was asked to tour the districts located in the Hyderabad-Karnataka area and Shimoga district to make election assessment, assembly segment wise. I visited all the districts assigned to me quite frequently, met various sections of society and tried to feel the pulse of the people of those districts.

I did my assessment in a systematic manner. As caste composition of a constituency matters a lot in elections, I collected the percentage of voters belonging to different castes in the constituencies. I also studied the results of the previous assembly and Parliamentary elections to get an indication regarding the voters' behaviour in the past. I would collect information on what basis the voters made their choice – whether the priority was the party or the individual candidate. I would talk to SHOs of each and every police station in the district and get his/her opinion of the probable winners. Similarly, I would talk to leaders of political parties, journalists, etc, and get an indication. I would specifically talk to teachers as they would give a valuable input about the mood of the electorate.

Later on, I would talk to opinion leaders in the constituency as well as a cross section of the electorate and come to my own logical conclusion. Though such assessments may not be as scientific as they are being done nowadays, we would definitely know which way the wind was blowing.

Most political parties valued the opinion of the Intelligence department as they thought that the police officers know the pulse of the people. It is a different matter that some officers, just to be in the good books of the political bosses fudge their report and give a rosy picture.

When the filing of nomination papers began, I learnt that the CM Gundu Rao had decided to contest from Chitapur in Gulbarga district apart from his own constituency of Somwarpet in Kodagu district. This was probably because Gulbarga district was considered a bastion of the Congress party at that time and hence 'safe' for the Chief Minister. I, therefore, went to Gulbarga once again and made a detailed assessment of Chitapur constituency. I reported that the CM would win by a thumping majority. However, the CM withdrew his nomination from Chitapur all of a sudden, that too in the last minute. On learning this, I met Kaarthikeyan and told him that a blunder was being committed. He told me that the CM didn't want to give an impression to the public that he was unsure of winning in his own constituency of Somwarpet.

An incumbent Chief Minister contesting an election from two constituencies would have definitely given an impression to the public that the CM was not sure of getting elected from his home constituency. But most Chief Ministers want to play safe. For example, during the 2018 assembly elections in Karnataka the incumbent CM, Siddaramaiah contested from two constituencies. While he lost from his own home constituency, he won from Badami in Bagalkot district. In the same elections, would-be Chief Minister HD Kumaraswamy contested from both Ramanagaram and Channapattana and won both. Earlier, his father Deve Gowda had contested for Parliament from Kanakapura and Hassan.

A reason that can be attributed is the vulnerability of many prominent politicians of facing electoral defeat. Any number of people, less from opposition parties and more from the same political party would be working behind the scenes to unseat the incumbent CM. Contesting from two constituencies would be an insurance against such attempts, I thought.

I was aware that a senior colleague of mine who was given the responsibility of making the electoral assessment of the four districts in the Mysore Division had reported that from Somwarpet constituency, Gundu Rao would win by a thumping margin. When I candidly said that the CM should not have withdrawn his nomination from Chitapur, Kaarthikeyan asked me to go to Somwarpet immediately and give my assessment about the electoral prospects of the CM. I travelled extensively and gathered information that Gundu Rao was unlikely to win as his voters perceived that he had not done much to the constituency as the Chief Minister. His close opponent Jivijaya of the Janata Party was preferred. There was a strong wind blowing in favour of the Janata Party in the taluk. When I submitted this report, DIG Kaarthikeyan appeared to be shocked and asked me many questions as to how I could come to such a conclusion. I gave my reasons. I was told that the DIG shared my assessment with the CM later.

Agile Indira Gandhi

Meanwhile, we were told that Prime Minister Indira Gandhi would extensively campaign for her party in Karnataka and we were asked to plan her tour accordingly. My colleague and former boss KR Srinivasan and I sat together to prepare her itinerary in consultation with the local officers and the Air Force as she had desired to travel by helicopter. The mandate given to us was to make her visit as many constituencies as possible within the given time frame.

After the plan we made was vetted by the CM, we sent it to the PM's office where with minor changes, the proposed programme was approved. We were told that the State Intelligence had to take care of the Prime Minister's proximate security. Those days there was no special unit like the SPG

(Special Protection Group), no black cat commandos to take care of the personal security of very important persons. Except for one officer from the VIP Security Wing of the Intelligence Bureau, and the Personal Security Officer of the PM, none would accompany the PM from Delhi. Hence we had to provide for security officers for her proximate security wherever she went in the State. The Special Protection Group was constituted to give proximate security to the Prime Minister only after the assassination of Indira Gandhi. While it performs inner ring security and bodyguard duties for the Prime Minister, the local police provide the second and third rings of security.

We roped in all the young and fit SPs and DySPs working in the State Intelligence for this work. I was given the task of taking care of her security in almost one-third of the places which she visited. My training in VIP Security for NAM Summit probably was a factor in this decision. I was allowed to travel in the escort helicopter and the escort cars of the Prime Minister. I covered Belgaum, Dharwad, Shimoga, Raichur, Bellary, Tumkur and Bangalore districts during these trips.

The drill was that whenever Mrs Gandhi got down from her helicopter, she would board an open jeep which would take her around the helipad perimeter and then on to the venue of the public meeting. I had to remain by her side in this vehicle along with her personal security officer who had come with her from Delhi. I remember an instance in Belgaum where I prevented the local MP from boarding the open jeep and coming near her. Only later I was told that the individual was the Member of Parliament, B Shankarananda whom I had not met or seen from close quarters earlier. I had in fact done my duty. I had similarly stopped a young well-dressed woman from approaching the PM near the public function venue at Shimoga. The then SP of the district Dr Ajai Kumar Singh had told me that she was IAS officer Anita (later Anita Kaul), the then Assistant Commissioner in the district and had asked me to allow her to meet the PM. I saw Anita give a written representation to the PM. I was told that it had something to do with her posting to Karnataka cadre.

I cannot forget an incident that took place in Sindhanur in Raichur district during the PM's visit. By the time the PM completed her public meeting, it was quite dark. She sat in the rear seat of the private car along with CM Gundu Rao and her personal security officer sat in the front seat. The car in which the PM was travelling belonged to HG Ramulu, then a Congress MP from Koppal parliamentary constituency. As the PM was addressing election meetings during that visit, she had preferred not to use government vehicles as far as possible.

As the PM's car moved forward, I ran to board the escort car in which my team and I were travelling. My car was immediately behind the PM's car. As I was getting into my car, I heard the sound of shattering glass. I immediately got out of my car and saw that the PM's car had stopped. I realized that a brick had been hurled at the PM's car breaking its rear windscreen.

Fortunately, nothing had happened to the PM or the CM. All of us were shocked at this sudden incident. We told Mrs Gandhi that she should shift to the VIP spare car in the convoy, but she smiled and told us not to worry and decided to proceed on the hour-long road journey to Bellary in the same car. I could not but admire her equanimity and courage.

Considering the seriousness of the incident, an enquiry was ordered. I do not remember at this time whether anyone was arrested or prosecuted for the offence. I only remember that my batch-mate Neelam Achuta Rao was the SP of Raichur district then.

I had also learnt that the PM was a frugal eater and most of the time she would make good with fruits and nuts for her breakfast or lunch. We would stock her helicopter with dry fruits, apples, bananas, fruit juices, biscuits, water bottles etc, so that the PM and her co-passengers, including the helicopter crew, could manage the long hours of travel. I came to know during this tour that every Tuesday, the PM would be fasting and would eat only boiled potatoes with curds.

Once after a long and tiring journey, we went to a roadside government guest house in Nelamangala of Bangalore Rural district for freshening up. While the PM used one room, all others who were accompanying her were huddled in the only other room of the guest house having their tea. I was standing in front of the PM's room. When she came out, she asked me about the CM and I told her that he was having his tea. Her attention was drawn towards the foundation stone of the guest house and on seeing that it was built over a century ago, asked me about the history of the town. Before I could say something, the other leaders rushed towards us and we proceeded on our road journey. I was amazed that she was so much interested in history.

When we attended a public meeting at Pavagada (a taluk in Tumkur bordering Andhra Pradesh), she had asked me about the 'wolf scare' in that town. At that time, a number of young children sleeping either in the open or in their huts had mysteriously disappeared and that people believed that a wolf was responsible for this. Unfortunately, the mystery was never solved. I wondered how the PM of the nation could remember such minor things!

During these visits, I marvelled at her inexhaustible source of energy. I never saw her exhausted even once. She would always keep a smiling face. I was told that she would do her paperwork after her dinner.

The elections concluded peacefully and all eyes were on the counting centres. We had asked an official of the Intelligence Wing to be present in each of the counting centres in all the districts and communicate to us the results through wireless after each round of counting. Those days we didn't have 24×7 television channels or cell phones and had to entirely depend on the Telecom Department or police wireless.

All eyes were on the counting centre at Somwarpet. IM Vittala Murthy, the Assistant Commissioner of Kodagu was the Returning Officer. Even after the results of many other constituencies were announced there was no news from the constituency from where the CM was contesting. At State Intelligence Headquarters we had become jittery. Soon it was obvious that the CM was trailing behind and when the results were declared, Jivijaya had secured about 5,000 votes more than the CM and was declared elected. It was also ironical that in Chitapur too which was a Congress stronghold, Vishwanath Patil Hebbal of the Janata Party had defeated his Congress rival Prabhakar Telkar by over 9,000 votes.

No party got a clear majority in the elections. While the Janata Party with 95 seats secured the first position, the Congress with 82 seats came second. A large number of Independents (22) had been elected. The moment results became public, CM Gundu Rao decided to tender his resignation.

Soon after this decision was known, Kaarthikeyan took all the SPs working in State Intelligence Headquarters to the CM's residence to bid him farewell and convey our gratitude. He was sitting in his room on the first floor. He shook hands with each one of us and on seeing me he said, "you were bold enough to state that I would lose in Somwarpet. But my friend sitting in the other room advised me otherwise. We didn't give much credence to your assessment thinking you to be a novice." While going downstairs, I peeped into the other room to see CM's friend FM Khan sitting in a sombre mood.

Very soon Ramakrishna Hegde formed the new government. We all knew that including Kaarthikeyan, DIG Intelligence, all the senior officers working in the State Intelligence Wing would be transferred as was the usual practice whenever a new government took charge. It happened sooner than later. Almost all the senior officers were posted out. I was transferred and posted as SP of Kodagu district. Jivijaya, who had defeated Gundu Rao, became a minister.

A few weeks after I reported for duty as Superintendent of Police, Kodagu district, Gundu Rao visited the district. I thought it was my duty to call on him and met him at the Government Guest House, Madikeri. Courtesy demanded that an ex-Chief Minister was met by the District Superintendent of Police. The former CM briefed me a lot of things about the district and the people of Kodagu which became very valuable indeed.

The next day a local newspaper reported that I had called on the ex-Chief Minister. This caused a big furore. Jivijaya and several workers of the Janata Party took strong exception to my meeting the ex-CM and calling me a stooge of Gundu Rao complained to Chief Minister Hegde to transfer me out of the district. I was told that the then District President of Janata Party, Ajjikuttira Somaiah prevailed upon his party leaders not to give too much of importance to this incident and put an end to the controversy. I remained as SP of Kodagu district only for twelve months. During this period Jivijaya and I had a good rapport and in the later years, he was quite friendly to me.

I was transferred to Gulbarga as SP in April 1984. When I was working as SP Gulbarga I tried to go on deputation to Government of India to work in an organization related to Intelligence and Security. After the assassination of Indira Gandhi in 1984, a new organization - Special Protection Group - was being formed to take care of the proximate security of the Prime Minister and applications had been called from officers of the level of SP to join. I applied for the post of Asst Director without any hesitation. The Director-designate of the new organization, Dr Subramanyam called me for an interview. I was not considered for the post for the sole reason that at that time I had a prominent paunch which made the interviewers feel that I was not physically fit enough to be given the challenging assignment. I felt quite disheartened and decided to do something about getting back to shape.

Because of my desire to go on deputation to work in Government of India, my name was being circulated to various Central Government organisations. Very soon I was picked to work in the Central Industrial Security Force. Those days CISF was not so huge or famous as it has become now. I was reluctant to join this organization and I tried very hard to get my name considered by the Central Intelligence Bureau instead. I didn't know at that time that once a Central organisation selects an officer, he/she cannot be considered by other Central organisations. I tried to extricate myself by trying with the State Government to cancel my deputation, but here again, I failed.

While working in the CISF at Delhi, I concentrated on my physical fitness and used to jog more than fifteen kilometres a day. I also used to meet officers of the Special Protection Group very frequently. Bobby Nair (Balachandran) of Tamil Nadu cadre was my neighbour in the government apartment block where I lived. Another officer from Tamil Nadu, K Vijay Kumar and I had done security duties during Non-Aligned Meet earlier. T Madiyal from Karnataka cadre was working as Dy Director of SPG at that time and we used to meet in his office every Friday for lunch. During one such meeting, I met the Director SPG and expressed my eagerness to join SPG. He readily agreed to consider my request. Due to my strict exercise regimen, I had lost my paunch and was quite fit to take up that assignment.

The Secretary Security who was in-charge of recruiting senior officers to the SPG called me for the final interview. He was none other than TN Seshan, IAS, who later became very famous as the Chief Election Commissioner of India. I was fortunate to come up to his expectations and he cleared my induction to SPG. Since I was working in the CISF and was to be transferred to the SPG, my file had to be cleared by the Ministry of Personnel. When my file reached that department, the Establishment Officer raised an objection that as I had already completed one year of my mandated four years of deputation with the Government of India. I could not serve the SPG for more than three years. This was not agreeable to either the SPG or to me and I had to remain content continuing to work with the CISF.

Working for four years in the CISF literally changed my world-view. Till I went to Delhi my world was Karnataka and its districts. As an IPS officer, I had a very cosy life in the districts. In Delhi, I did not have an official vehicle and had to travel to office and back using public transport. I was given a transit accommodation flat which was less than 700 sqft in area. Getting school admission for my son was a herculean task. Life used to be a big struggle. As an IPS officer in Karnataka, I had been pampered. In Delhi, I experienced the life of a commoner. There were hundreds of IPS officers working in Delhi and I was a junior among them. But living a hard life changed my perspective on various things completely and I thank my stars for giving me an opportunity to serve with the Government of India and get a better world-view.

In the CISF, probably due to my work ethics, I quickly gained a good reputation. I was first posted as a Staff Officer to the DIG of Northern Range who controlled CISF units in entire North India. Later I was given the all-important position of looking after the HR work of such a big organization. For the first time in my life, I came to view things with a pan-India perspective. During my stint in CISF, I travelled to virtually all the States of India and learnt so much about my country. After four years of work in Delhi, my term of the deputation was coming to an end.

In April 1990, I got a call that the Chief Minister of Karnataka Veerendra Patil, was camping in Delhi and that he had desired to see me. I went to the Karnataka Bhavan where he was staying. PP Prabhu, the Principal Secretary to the CM took me to the suite of the CM and introduced me. The CM said that he had known about me as I had served as SP of Gulbarga district. (He was a Union Minister then.) Prabhu told the CM that I was completing my deputation tenure and I was to be promoted in the State to the rank of a DIG and suggested to the CM that I could be considered for posting as Deputy Inspector General of Police, North-Eastern Range, Gulbarga. The CM looked at me for my reaction. I told him that I would deem it a great honour to work in the Range which covers the home district of the CM. He smiled and shook hands with me.

Within a very short period, I received my promotion-cum-posting order as the DIG of Gulbarga which covered Bidar, Gulbarga, and Raichur districts. Gulbarga and Raichur had not been bifurcated then.

I returned to Karnataka in May 1990 on promotion but had no chance of calling on the CM after assumption of my new post. The first time I met him after coming back to the State was in July.

Bidar Blast

On July 12, there was a bomb blast in a cinema hall, Deepak theatre, in Bidar town in which scores of people had been killed. On coming to know of this ghastly incident I rushed to Bidar and directly went to the crime scene. Blood and flesh were sticking to the walls of the cinema hall and the entire area was reeking of burnt flesh. Severed human limbs had been scattered on the seats, on the aisle, and on the floor. An Improvised Explosive Device had been placed below the seat at the rear portion of the hall and the explosion had taken place about ten minutes after the interval. We surmised that the terrorists who had brought the crude bomb had left the hall during the interval after triggering the device.

It was evident that the blast in the theatre was the consequence of the massacre of Sikh students in Bidar town during the anti-Sikh riots in September 1988. Bidar was a sacred place of pilgrimage to the Sikhs as Guru Nanak Maharaj had visited the town in the 16th century and had alleviated the acute drinking water problem of the local populace by making a spring of water emerge. A Gurudwara had later been built at the spot and many Sikhs came to live in Bidar. Consequent to the establishment of an engineering college, a good number of Sikh students were studying in Bidar and in the riots of 1988 six of them had lost their lives.

A large number of persons injured in the cinema hall blast had been admitted to the District Hospital and many had died on their way to the Hospital. Establishing the identity of the deceased was a tough task. I summoned officers and men from Gulbarga and Raichur districts to help the Bidar district police in this task. Since this attack, probably the very first terror attack in Karnataka, was perceived to be an act of revenge for the killing of Sikh students in Bidar town in 1988, we had to be extra vigilant to prevent communal backlash against the Sikhs. I camped in Bidar that night.

The very next morning I heard that the CM Veerendra Patil, would be arriving at Bidar. I received him at the State border and briefed him about the incident. After visiting the cinema hall he went to the District Hospital and spoke to the injured. Later on, he addressed the officers and gave directions about dealing with the possible repercussions. He separately addressed leaders of various communities and political parties and sought their help in maintaining peace and communal harmony in the district. He held a press conference subsequently and announced handing over the investigation of the case to the Corps of Detectives (CoD). Marvelling at the calm and composed way he handled the situation, I felt that he was a statesman.

In the later weeks, our meetings were restricted to his visit to Gulbarga which was rare. Once I called on him at his residence and briefed him about the law and order situation in the range. He heard me patiently, asked a few questions and concluded the meeting.

Till he was in office, he never interfered with the working of the police. Not a single phone call he had made to me. Those days I felt that the CM worked more like a bureaucrat than a politician. It was quite tragic that he was eased out from his office in October 1990 under unfortunate circumstances.

Adamant VP Singh

During my tenure as the DIG of Gulbarga Range, I had an opportunity to handle several VIP visits. The visit of Prime Minister Chandra Shekhar to Gulbarga city is one such visit etched in my memory. The PM was to address a public meeting in the police parade grounds and we had got the helipad constructed adjacent to these grounds. Elaborate security arrangements had been made by the district administration. While the organisers had expected huge crowds to attend, the number of people in the parade ground hardly exceeded 300.

We received the PM at the helipad. He was accompanied by Dr Subramanian Swamy. He came to the meeting venue and began speaking. After a few minutes, there was power failure and the loudspeakers became silent. Arrangements had been made for alternative power supply, but these too failed and the amplifiers refused to come to life. The PM became visibly irritated by this turn of events. A police officer lent him a hand-held hailer to use. Instead of speaking from the podium, the PM went close to the crowd and began speaking. When the Additional DGP, Law and Order, who had come to Gulbarga to supervise the security arrangements, advised the PM not to go too close to the crowd in the interest of security, the PM lost his cool and shouted at the officer. He (the PM) soon left the venue in a huff. After his helicopter took off, his supporters took to stone-throwing in which the District Magistrate received a minor injury.

VP Singh, who had demitted office as the Prime Minister in 1990 visited Koppal in the then Raichur district to canvass for his party candidate Siddaramaiah who was contesting the 1991 Lok Sabha elections. As the Range DIG, I went to Koppal to supervise the security arrangements. When the election meeting concluded it was quite dark. The ex-PM was to go to Raichur by road, stay overnight and leave for Hyderabad the next day. After a long drive, we reached Raichur at around 10 PM. VP Singh had wanted to stay in the Inspection Bungalow at Raichur. The SP told him that as the IB was not found suitable for his stay from the security point of view, arrangements had been made in the Karnataka Power Corporation Guest House at Shakti Nagar located about 20 km away. He grudgingly continued the road journey.

When Singh got down from his car at the Shakti Nagar Guest House, he went to his room in a hurry and after some time sat for his dinner. At that time one of his aides met me and told me that the ex-PM had decided to proceed to Hyderabad and camp there. As I was telling the aide that it would not be possible, Singh himself came to me and asked the reason. I told him that we were at the border of Andhra Pradesh and as Karnataka Police didn't have jurisdiction in Andhra Pradesh, we could not allow him to travel without arranging for his security. I also told him that the route to Hyderabad passed through Naxal areas, and hence it would be better if he performed the journey the next day. He flared up at me for not agreeing to his request and rushed back to his room.

After a few minutes, his assistant again met me and stated that the ex-PM had contacted the Governor of Andhra Pradesh and that he would be staying at Raj Bhavan, Hyderabad for the night. He told me that VP Singh was very adamant and had decided to go to Hyderabad even without taking any security detail. I immediately contacted the police control room, Andhra Pradesh and conveyed the news. I asked the Andhra police to take care of the security of the ex-PM during his ensuing road journey. Knowing quite well that it would be extremely difficult for Andhra Pradesh police to take care of the ex-PM's security at such a short notice, I sent an escort party from Raichur district to go with the ex-PM's convoy up to Hyderabad. Only after I received the news that the ex-PM had reached Hyderabad safely I could go to sleep. While I could understand the reason for the Prime Minister Chandra Shekhar to flare up at the police, I could not even guess why VP Singh had flared up at me.

Sportive Rajiv Gandhi

Ex-PM Rajiv Gandhi came to Bidar to address an election rally on May 14, 1991. He had come in a special private aircraft which had landed at the Air Force base in Bidar. The election rally was held at a ground close to the Air Force Station. Though it was quite late in the night, a large number of people had gathered to listen to him. A highlight of this meeting was the recital of a poem in Urdu hailing Rajiv Gandhi composed and read by Mohsin Kamal, ex-MLA. I have already mentioned about Kamal who was the Congress candidate for the bye-election to Bidar Assembly constituency in 1982. The ex-PM was quite pleased with Kamal.

As he was boarding his aircraft, I went to bid him goodbye along with the SP, Bidar. Shaking hands with me, he took me aside and thanked me for the *bandobust* arrangements made. He asked me about the law and order situation in the Range and when I replied that it was quite peaceful, he told me to ensure that no trouble takes place during the elections.

Exactly a week later, when I got a message that Rajiv Gandhi had been assassinated at Sriperumbadur in Tamil Nadu, I could not believe my ears.

I am tempted to recount my brief meetings with him earlier when I had worked as the SP of Gulbarga district.

In February 1985, Rajiv Gandhi had visited Gulbarga to address an election meeting at the police parade ground. He had assumed the office of the Prime Minister only a few months earlier. Immediately after concluding his speech, he desired to leave for Hyderabad by road. I told him that the road journey would take almost 4 hours and requested him to relax for a few minutes in a nearby guest-room named after his brother Sanjay Gandhi.

During his visit to Gulbarga earlier, Sanjay Gandhi had rested for a while in a guest-room located in the pavilion adjacent to the police parade ground and hence the room was known as 'Sanjay Gandhi Room'. When I was a probationer in Gulbarga district, I had stayed in that room for more than 3 months.

The Prime Minister stated that he was in a hurry to leave and declined to rest for a while. We managed to offer him a tender coconut which he accepted gratefully. He chatted with Mallikarjuna Kharge, Dharam Singh and the other Congress candidates for the Assembly elections for a few minutes and left the venue.

I had hurriedly arranged a pilot vehicle for the PM's convoy which was being driven by an Asst Sub-Inspector. I had decided to go in the escort car up to our district border near Humnabad. As the VIP vehicle started moving, I noticed that the Prime Minister himself was sitting in the driver's seat. After we left the outskirts of the city I realised that the PM wanted the pilot vehicle to move faster. I communicated this to the pilot car through wireless but got a reply that as it was an old vehicle it couldn't move faster.

After we crossed the village Kamlapur, the pilot car was unable to climb the small hill road and was moving very slowly. The PM had become impatient and started honking furiously. But the police car couldn't match the speed of the PM's car. The PM overtook the pilot vehicle and started going ahead. I was worried because it was against the security drill. Besides, the PM didn't know the road. I made my car overtake the VIP vehicle and pilot it. At the border of Bidar district, the pilot vehicle of Bidar police took over and I was asked to continue my escort duty till the Andhra border. At the border, I went towards the VIP vehicle, saluted the PM and took his leave. He gave me a mischievous grin.

Rajiv Gandhi once again came to Gulbarga district in May 1985 to inspect certain drought relief works. He came in a helicopter and landed in a village in Afzalpur taluk. He was accompanied by Sonia Gandhi and Mani Shankar Aiyar. After we received him at the helipad, he expressed a desire to travel in an open jeep, to the spot where drought relief works were being taken up. The open jeep which the police had at the venue was meant for ceremonial purposes and was not fit to take the PM in the rough terrain. The PM insisted on riding that jeep. At one point where the jeep had difficulty in climbing, the PM asked the police driver to get down and allow him (the PM) to drive. I was very much concerned. Fortunately, the jeep climbed up in its second try and I had heaved a sigh of relief.

These thoughts came to my mind as I drove back to my office to plan for security arrangements to avoid the possible aftermath of the assassination. Thankfully my Range remained by and large peaceful.

Even to this day, the smiling face of Rajiv Gandhi keeps recurring in my mind.

After my return to the State as DIG and working in Gulbarga for a considerable period, I realized that my foray into Intelligence/Security establishments with the Government of India had virtually ended.

I had to wait for more than two decades to be back in Intelligence, but this time thankfully it was as the Head of State Intelligence in Karnataka.

3

Back to Intelligence Wing as Additional DGP

On April 10, 2003, when I received my posting orders as Additional DGP and Head of State Intelligence, I was surprised and also elated. The Intelligence Wing was directly reporting to the Chief Minister and the Home Minister who oversaw the working of the Police Department had no control over it. I knew that the choice of the officer to Head State Intelligence was made by the CM personally. It was a prestigious post and I was aware many of my seniors were trying for that post and had even lobbied for it.

When I was wondering, what might have prompted CM SM Krishna, to select me as his Chief of Intelligence, I presumed that my work as the Director of the State Information Department, a few years earlier, wherein the CM had directly seen my working, might have been the reason.

I had worked as the Director of Information from November 27, 1999 till June 6, 2002. I was not the first police officer in Karnataka to hold that post. PS Ramanujam, S Krishnamurthy, Vijay Sasanur, KVR Tagore and Subhash Bharani had earlier worked as heads of Information Department. Prof BK Chandrasekhar, who was the Minister in-Charge of that Department, had chosen me to Head the Department. I was told that he had chosen me on the advice of the then ADG Intelligence and former Director of Information Dr Ramanujam. I was then working in Karnataka Road

Transport Corporation as Director and Dr Ramanujam had known that I was a former journalist, albeit for a very short time, and was interested in media relations. The CM had given concurrence for this appointment. When the minister asked me whether I would like to be considered for the posting, I had willingly and happily agreed.

I had known that every Chief Minister gave a lot of importance to this Department as it was tasked to trumpet the various achievements of the government. For this reason, I had to interact with the CM very often. Being the Head of the Department meant that I was the bridge between the government and the media persons and hence I was quite sought after by both. Apart from media relations, the department also dealt with matters related to feature and documentary films.

I quickly got adjusted to the new Department. Within a few months of my taking over the reins of Department, I had overhauled its working which was appreciated both by the CM and the Information Minister. I had settled down in my job comfortably.

Rajkumar Abduction

This comfort was short-lived as a calamity happened by the end of July 2000. On July 31, around 4.30 AM, I got a call from Vijay Sasanur, who was then working as Addl DGP Administration in the office of the DGP. He informed me that Kannada film star Rajkumar has been kidnapped by notorious forest brigand Veerappan and that I had to organize a press meet within next three hours. He also mentioned that he was present at the residence of SM Krishna along with the DG and IGP, the Home Minister, and others. I was aware that Sasanur was very close to Dr Rajkumar, and hence I sought more details from him. He told me that the abduction took place the previous night around 10 PM from the farmhouse of the film actor in Chikka Gajanur village in Tamil Nadu. This village was situated at the border of Karnataka and Tamil Nadu and was close to Chamarajanagar in Karnataka. On hearing this, I remarked that we should thank our stars that it didn't happen in Karnataka which would have resulted in a major law and order problem for the State. Sasanur agreed with me and asked me to reach the CM's residence as soon as I could.

When I reached 'Anugraha', the official residence of the CM, everyone present there looked worried. I was told to get the press meet organized at the CM's home office 'Krishna' by 8 AM. Though media persons rarely attend any press meet before 11 AM, that day's press meet which began at 9 AM was jam-packed. SM Krishna read out a prepared statement detailing some facts about the abduction. Raghavendra Rajkumar, elder son of Dr Rajkumar, also made a statement to the media and appealed to the public to maintain peace. Soon after the press meet concluded, I went to my Minister Chandrasekhar and briefed him about the kidnapping and its imminent repercussions in the State.

Meanwhile, the Chief Minister left for Chennai along with many others and after his return to Bangalore in the evening, the CM called leaders of all the political parties for a meeting at Vidhana Soudha and briefed them about the incident and what was being done by the government. This was followed by a State Cabinet meeting. I was present in Vidhana Soudha and was asked by the CM to organize one more press briefing. Krishna informed the assembled media persons about his meeting with his counterpart in Tamil Nadu, Karunanidhi, and the efforts being made by the government to get the actor released unharmed by the bandit.

I had to be closely involved with this matter for two reasons. Dr Rajkumar was part and parcel of the film industry and all matters related to this industry came under the purview of the department I headed. Similarly, the abduction was a very important matter for the media and media relations was also the concern of my department. I had to, Therefore, know day to day happenings about the efforts made for the actor's safe release. Also being an IPS officer, I had a professional interest in the matter.

The assistance of the Information Department was soon sought by Parvatamma Rajkumar. She had realized that the actor was without his medications and wanted the abductors to know this fact. Thanks to the brilliant suggestion of my colleague in the Information Department, DP Murlidhar, we asked the lady to make an appeal on an audio tape which we got the All India Radio to broadcast. At that time it was known that Veerappan was in the habit of listening to the radio. Such assistance of our Department was used twice during the period of abduction.

On September 8, 2000, Karunanidhi, the CM of Tamil Nadu, arrived in Bangalore for a meeting with SM Krishna. I was informed that after the meeting, both would jointly address a press conference in Vidhana Soudha. I made preparations for the same and attended the conference. Karunanidhi assured that Tamil Nadu was sparing no efforts to get the actor released early. I was appreciative of the deft way in which Karunanidhi handled the most uncomfortable and embarrassing questions posed to him by the media. Karunanidhi spoke to the media in Tamil. As many journalists who were present could understand that language, no problem arose. For those who didn't understand what he spoke, one of the aides of Karunanidhi translated it in English.

On September 29, I learnt that Nagappa Maradagi, an assistant director of feature films and one of the persons taken hostage by Veerappan along with Dr Rajkumar, had escaped from custody and had returned to Bangalore. On getting the information that he was sitting in the CM's home office, I went there. Nagappa had already met the CM and had briefed him about the episode. I told the officers present there that the media is very keen to know how Nagappa escaped the clutches of Veerappan and also about the welfare of Dr Rajkumar. I suggested that we should allow Nagappa to address the media. This was agreed to.

Though the press meet was almost sudden, the conference room of the CM's home office 'Krishna' was brimming with media persons. Nagappa met the press and answered a barrage of questions. I found him to be theatrical in his interaction with the media and got an impression that even the media persons did not buy his story.

Nakkeeran Gopal, the intermediary of both the governments to negotiate with Veerappan, confirmed the story of Nagappa. But Veerappan's silence over this episode in the tapes he subsequently sent to the governments was intriguing. Nagappa had told me much later that he was very much pained to hear people say that by his escape he had endangered the life of Dr Rajkumar.

On October 16, Veerappan released Rajkumar's son-in-law Govindaraju. I met him too at CM's residence and learnt more about Veerappan and his activities in the forest.

Though at that time I was functioning as the Head of the State Information Department, I was not entrusted with the work of briefing the media on behalf of the government. My role was restricted to organizing press meets. In fact, those days even the Chief Minister and the Home Minister Mallikarjuna Kharge exercised great restraint in talking about this episode to the media. I remember the DG and IGP C Dinakar briefing the media occasionally about the efforts being made by Karnataka to get the actor released. My former colleague KR Srinivasan was also involved in talking to the Tamil Nadu Police and the government, but he too would not address the media.

On the evening of November 14, there were rumours that Dr Rajkumar had been released by Veerappan. My efforts to get this confirmed ended in vain. The next day, however, an official announcement was made that the actor was released in the morning and that he would be arriving in Bangalore the next day.

On coming to know of this, I briefed the Chief Minister about the need to organize a press meet and told him that we would organize it in the conference hall in Vidhana Soudha. He agreed to this suggestion. Right from ten in the morning, I got the seating arrangement in the hall rearranged. I thought that by doing so, we could accommodate a large number of media persons. I had been flooded with requests by media persons for passes to attend this important press meet. A large number of media representatives from foreign media too attended.

On his arrival at the airport, Dr Rajkumar was brought in a car to Vidhana Soudha. He was accompanied by his family members. Conspicuous by their presence were Dr (?) Bhanu, who reportedly negotiated with Veerappan for the release of the actor, and Kempaiah, an IPS officer very close to the actor.

They all sat in the head table along with the CM, Dr Rajkumar, the DG and IGP, and others. Dr Rajkumar looked as though he had aged considerably. Though he was cheerful, I could observe that the 108-day ordeal had taken a toll on his health. He was tired. He expressed his gratitude to all those who helped him. What surprised me was that he didn't express any rancour towards Veerappan and had some good words for him. I thought this to be the result of Stockholm syndrome.

During the press conference, I observed Dr Bhanu hovering around Dr Rajkumar and the actor describing her as an 'angel'. On seeing her, I recollected that a few years ago a businessman dealing in marbles, Davide, from Carrara in Italy, had met me and had told me that he had given a complaint to the police against Bhanu for cheating him in a business deal and had sought my help. I had put in a word to the jurisdictional police and had forgotten about the episode.

On my enquiries after the press conference, I was told that Bhanu owned a granite quarry in Chamarajanagar district. I was not made aware of how and why she was involved in the efforts to release Dr Rajkumar and what role she had actually played in getting the film star released.

After Dr Rajkumar addressed the media, the reporters present asked him many questions, but I thought that the actor was not answering them logically. He appeared to be dazed. This was realized by the Chief Minister Krishna and he ended the conference. Many questions had remained unanswered.

Except for those 30 months in the State Information Department, I had no occasion to come in close contact with the CM for him to choose me as his Head of Intelligence. I had also not been close to any politician for someone to recommend my name. In fact, I had remained away from politics and politicians as I had been trained that as a public servant and also as a police officer, my allegiance was only to the Indian Constitution and not to any political personage. Except for a short stint as SP Intelligence over two decades ago, I had not done much Intelligence work either and I wondered whether I would do justice to the job I was entrusted with. I was the junior most officer in the Addl DGP rank then. Therefore, I had been surprised at getting the post of Addl DG Intelligence.

Though the CM had reposed confidence in selecting me for such a sensitive post, my mind was filled with doubts. Hence I called on the DG and IGP T Madiyal, in the evening to seek his advice. Madiyal had earlier headed the State Intelligence when Veerappa Moily was the CM. He had also worked in the Special Protection Group overseeing the security of the Prime Minister of India. Asking me not to have self-doubts, he gave me valuable tips and directed me to take charge of my new assignment the very next day.

On April 11, which happened to be the auspicious *Rama Navami*, I assumed charge of my new post. When I called on the CM at his residence, he told me that he had selected me because he found me to keep a low profile and being focussed in my work. Thanking him for the confidence reposed in me, I assured him that I would work hard to come up to his expectations. I was determined to succeed in the job that I loved to do.

The State Intelligence was then headed by an Additional DGP who was assisted by an IGP and a DIGP in the headquarters. There were half a dozen Superintendents of Police in the Headquarters. One of them was exclusively meant for the security of the CM. In each police range in the State, an SP Intelligence had been posted. We had adequate number of support staff.

It was the tradition in Karnataka that the Head of Intelligence met the CM the first thing every morning and brief him about all important happenings in the State and the country. The CM used to be seen off and received at the airport whenever he would travel outside Bangalore by the ADG Intelligence. I followed this tradition.

A month into my new job, I felt that Krishna was not attaching any importance for my daily briefings. I would religiously arrive at his official residence, 'Anugraha', around seven in the morning and intimate his attendants about my arrival. I would wait to meet him in the office room which was on the ground floor. The residential portion of the CM's house was in the first floor and the rear portion of the ground floor consisted of the kitchen and dining hall. There were two side entrances to the building, one near the staircase and the other near the kitchen.

During the first few days, Krishna would come to his office room and listen to my briefing for a few minutes and conclude the meeting. Most of the times, he would not react to whatever I reported. If at all he reacted, it was in monosyllables. I felt this to be strange. As SP in the Intelligence Wing earlier, I had seen my DIG Kaarthikeyan, spend hours with the then Chief Minister Gundu Rao and had known that the DIG would be consulted by the CM for almost every major decision.

Sometimes while I was waiting in his office room to brief him, I would be told that the CM had already left home and gone towards his home office 'Krishna'. The buildings, 'Anugraha' and 'Krishna', were located side by side. The CM would exit 'Anugraha' from its back door, walk a hundred yards and using a wicket gate, would enter his home office 'Krishna'.

When this happened the first time, I went to his office room in 'Krishna' to brief him. The CM had already closeted himself with a visitor and I saw a large number of visitors waiting outside to meet him. I had to wait for more than an hour to meet the CM and brief him. This resulted in upsetting my office schedule. Hence, I decided not to give the CM a chance to go to 'Krishna' without meeting me. I would sit near a window from where I could watch the walkway between both the buildings and the moment I saw the CM walking towards his home office without seeing me, I would sprint out of 'Anugraha' and catch him before he reached the wicket gate. It was like a cat and mouse game. Most of the security guards posted would have a hearty laugh seeing me run to catch the CM.

Concerned about the CM's disinterest in getting the Intelligence briefing the first thing in the morning, I sought the advice of two of my predecessors who had worked with SM Krishna. They told me that the CM might have felt that I was not giving him any useful information which he had not known already through other sources.

It was a common talk those days that my second-in-command, IG Intelligence T Jayaprakash, was very close to the CM and had gained the CM's trust. Jayaprakash, whose mother Smt BL Subbamma was twice elected Congress MLA from Chikmagalur, had a direct channel of communication with the CM and his family. While Mrs Krishna hailed from Shimoga district bordering Chikmagalur, the CM's first son-in-law belonged to Chikmagalur district. Jayaprakash had been working as the IG Intelligence ever since SM Krishna had assumed office as the Chief Minister, whereas I was the third ADG Intelligence after Krishna took office. I had noticed that the CM was more at ease with Jayaprakash and would communicate his orders to others through him quite frequently.

I thought over this matter deeply. It was a fact that most of the information I was giving to the CM would already have been reported to him through the Daily Situation Report which my office was sending to the CM every night. Secondly, the electronic and print media would have covered the major incidents that had happened in the State and the country. I therefore, thought that whatever I reported to him should be something which kindled his interest and which was not stale.

While I was wondering how to go about it, an opportunity came my way on May 23. The CM wanted me to find about the alleged kidnapping of a prominent Congress worker JN Metgud from Belgaum district, by persons close to the then Agriculture Minister VS Koujalgi. Koujalgi, an MLA from Arabhavi constituency in Belgaum district, had earlier been the President of Karnataka Pradesh Congress Committee and had to resign in 2001 following a 'sting' operation allegedly showing him accepting money for getting a work done in Belgaum Zilla Panchayat office. On getting a clean chit from the Lokayukta, he had been inducted into the cabinet as Agriculture Minister only a few weeks ago.

Rumours were afloat then that a former President of National Students' Union of India, and an active party worker JN Metgud was in possession of a fresh tape involving the Minister and that Metgud had been kidnapped when he was returning to Belgaum after meeting the CM in Bangalore and tortured to return the tape. Satish Jarkiholi, the then MLC of Janata Dal (Secular) had written to the CM requesting a probe by a Central agency. Jarkiholi had also claimed that he had a copy of the said tape. Krishna, on receipt of the letter from the MLC, had asked me to probe the matter.

My enquiries revealed that Metgud was a member of a group of Congressmen inimical to Koujalgi. A follower of Koujalgi had initiated a criminal case against Metgud. This had deepened the fissure between both the groups resulting in allegations and counter allegations against each other. It appeared that both groups wanted to establish political supremacy in Gokak taluka. None of the *dramatis personae* was willing to talk when I conducted my enquiry. I presumed that certain damage control measures might have been taken by the concerned. Though I had a suspicion that the allegation was true, as no proof was forthcoming, I had to report to the CM that there was no substance in the allegation made by the MLC. Very soon the matter died down.

On July 5, I learnt from the Police Commissioner Hubli that the CM had landed there in a special aircraft and had left for a surprise inspection of Naragund and Navalgund talukas. He stated that the Principal Secretary to the CM, K Jairaj, and IGP T Jayaprakash, were accompanying the CM. I was terribly embarrassed because as ADG in-charge of the CM's security, I was not aware of the CM's movements and also had to learn about the CM's tour through secondary sources. Moreover, I was actually proceeding to Hubli by road on official work the same day and had indeed taken the CM's permission for this trip. On my return to Bangalore, I questioned the Principal Secretary as well as the IGP, Intelligence for keeping me in the dark about the CM's tour. Both replied that the CM had desired to keep this visit a secret from everyone.

A few days earlier too I had faced a similar situation when I came to know about the expansion of the State Cabinet only through the Special Officer to the Home Minister and not through anyone from CM's office.

As the Head of Intelligence, I had to interact almost on a day-to-day basis with the officials of the Chief Minister's Secretariat apart from the Chief Secretary, the Home Secretary, Secretary in-charge of Protocol and the DG and IGP. Occasionally I had also to meet the Governor of Karnataka to whom I had to send a report concerning law and order matters of the State.

The Chief Minister's office was headed by a Principal Secretary who was assisted by two Secretaries, all of whom were IAS officers. When I became the ADG Intelligence, my batch-mate Jairaj was working as the Principal Secretary. Prior to him, SV Ranganath was the Principal Secretary and when he went on Central deputation, Jairaj had been posted to the CM's Secretariat. The Secretary-1 was MK Shankaralinge Gowda, who like Jayaprakash had been elevated to the All India Services from the State service. He had been the Secretary almost from the time Krishna assumed office as the CM. I had a feeling that Krishna trusted him more. The Secretary-2 was Jawaid Akhtar.

An officer of the Karnataka Administrative Service, Prakash, was the Officer on Special Duty (OSD) to the CM. His duties included preparation of the CM's daily schedules, arranging meetings and appointments for the CM, and generally work as a Personal Secretary. He had to be with the CM wherever the CM went and usually it was he who communicated the orders of the CM to the concerned from time to time. Shortly after I became the ADG Intelligence, BN Krishnaiah assumed charge as the OSD. I maintained excellent relations with all these officers whom I was meeting every day.

On July 10, when I found the CM in good mood, I mentioned about his Nargund visit and told him that I needed to be kept informed about his movements as I was responsible for his security. The CM simply smiled and nodded his head. On that day I resolved that I would work harder to gain the confidence of the CM and make myself wanted instead of getting a feeling of being left out of action.

Fortunately, the bye-elections to the State Legislature came in handy to prove my worth to the CM. The bye-elections were necessitated consequent to the death of the sitting MLAs SR Kashappanavar of Hungund in Bagalkot district and Byre Gowda of Vemagal in Kolar district. I had personally known Kashappanavar since my days as a DIG Gulbarga range.

In fact, it was I who had broken the news to the CM of the death of Kashappanavar, a former minister, who had died in a ghastly road accident near Kudligi in Bellary district around 3 AM on June 27. Having come to know of this within an hour of the incident, I had telephoned the CM very early in the morning and shared the news. Kashappanavar was earlier the Minister for Small Scale Industries in the State Cabinet of Krishna and had been dropped from the cabinet a year ago when the cabinet was reshuffled. Upset over this, the ex-minister was reported to have approached Sonia Gandhi and complained to her against the CM. This, I was told, had soured the relations between him and the CM. Later in the day when I met the CM for my daily briefing, I requested him to attend the funeral. The CM did attend.

When the bye-elections were announced, the CM entrusted me with the task of conducting a survey in both the constituencies and give a report about the mood of the electorate. In the first week of September, I travelled extensively in both the constituencies and personally made an assessment and reported that in both the constituencies the sympathy factor for the departed MLAs would play a major role and hence Gouramma Kashappanavar, wife of the late MLA and Krishna Byre Gowda, son of the late MLA would win. The election results announced on September 29 proved me right.

Later on, I was asked to assess the outcome of the elections to the Karnataka Legislative Council from the local body constituencies. As assessed by us, the Congress won with a thumping majority. After this, the CM appeared to have gained some confidence in my ability and started seeking my views on important matters. He had agreed to my request to post Auradkar as the DIG in the Intelligence Wing. He would listen to my briefings more patiently, ask questions, get his doubts clarified and also speak his mind. I was happy that at last, I was proving productive to the CM.

4

Stamp Paper Scam and Naxal Encounter

In the latter part of 2003, there was a growing demand that the investigation of the multi-billion rupee stamp paper scam, being conducted by the State police, be handed over to the CBI. The scam involved printing and distribution of fake stamp papers all over the country masterminded by Abdul Karim Lala Telgi. The scam had come to light three years earlier.

On August 19, 2000, Bangalore city police received information from an anonymous caller that two persons were carrying fake stamps on Subedar Chatram Road, an important road in Bangalore. A lookout was mounted and two persons who matched the description by the caller were apprehended. When searched, they were found to carry fake stamps and stamp papers and were unable to give satisfactory replies about the origin of the papers. A case was registered in Upparpet Police Station and based on the information given by the arrested persons, many more were arrested and fake stamp papers worth crores of rupees were seized. Considering the nature of the case, the government constituted a special investigation team, named STAMPIT, headed by Srikumar, an Additional DGP. Kumar, three years senior to me in the IPS, had earned a name as an ace investigator and had worked in the CBI and was also a part of the team that investigated Rajiv Gandhi assassination. He had done his work in a methodical manner.

STAMPIT, the Special Investigation Team of Srikumar, was on the lookout for the elusive Telgi, the kingpin of the racket. On receiving information that Telgi was based in Mumbai, a team of officers was sent to arrest him, but Telgi eluded them. They, however, arrested Telgi on November 7, 2001 from Ajmer in Rajasthan and brought him to Bangalore.

Son of a railway employee at Khanapur in Belgaum district of Karnataka, Telgi had started his life as a fruit vendor. He went to the Gulf and after working there for a few years returned to Mumbai and was doing some odd jobs. In 1993, he was arrested in a cheating case by the Mumbai police and while in custody he made friends with a Mumbai stockbroker Ram Ratan Soni who had been arrested in a fake share transfer case. Telgi learnt from Soni that counterfeiting stamp papers would be a very profitable business and both of them joined hands after their release to start the stamp paper business. Telgi acquired a licence to vend stamp papers in 1994. Befriending officials of the Security Press in Nashik, he began counterfeiting stamp papers and using his contacts with the bank and other officials he established a wide distribution network to distribute them all over the country. The very next year Soni and Telgi were arrested in a fake stamp paper case by Mumbai police. Telgi fell into the Karnataka Police net much later.

During the investigation of the case by Karnataka STAMPIT team, it was revealed that Telgi had sold fake stamp papers in many other States as well. Several politicians, bigwigs, and police officers were suspected to be involved in it. During his interrogation, lie detector as well as narco-analysis tests, Telgi had named many influential persons including politicians, senior government officials and police officers as being facilitators in his criminal venture.

After his arrest, Telgi had been lodged in Parappana Agrahara Central Prison in Bangalore and STAMPIT officers came to know that he was using several telephones even while in prison and had continued running his racket unabated. Tapping of his telephone conversations by the STAMPIT had revealed his nexus with influential people. In his telephone conversations, he had named a number of serving police officers of Karnataka, including a few IPS officers, to be close to him.

As the investigation progressed in several States in India against Telgi, there was a clamour for investigation of all the cases against him by a Central agency. Several petitions had also been filed in the Supreme Court for transfer of the cases to the CBI.

At that time in Karnataka, there was a growing suspicion that Roshan Baig, the Small Scale Industries Minister in the Cabinet of SM Krishna was close to Telgi. The Opposition parties had wanted action against Baig. On December 15, 2003, a city court had issued an arrest warrant against the Minister's brother Dr Rehan Baig in connection with this case. Five days later, Dr Baig surrendered before the investigation team. He claimed that he was innocent and that an attempt was being made to tarnish the image of his brother by the Minister's political opponents. As the demand for a probe by the CBI intensified, Chief Minister called Srikumar for a briefing about the case, I was also present during the briefing.

On December 23, 2003, the CM called me for a meeting at his residence. I found senior ministers Mallikarjuna Kharge and Dharam Singh sitting with the CM. The CM asked me to brief all of them about the Telgi case investigation and the feasibility of handing over of its further investigation to the CBI. Though I had no role to play in the investigation of this case, I was aware of the progress of the investigation. Raghavendra Auradkar, the then DIG Intelligence, had earlier worked in the STAMPIT team and had a thorough knowledge of the case. Besides, on many occasions when Srikumar briefed the progress of the investigation to the DG and IGP, I too would be present. Srikumar had also discussed the case in detail with me.

During the meeting chaired by the CM, I suggested that as the finger of suspicion was pointing towards a sitting Minister, it would be better if the case was handed over to the CBI. I opined that by handing it over to the CBI, the government would be giving an impression to the public that it had nothing to hide and that it was not trying to protect anyone. The two senior ministers present nodded their heads in agreement.

Later on, Srikumar's opinion was also sought. He was against handing over the case to anyone else as STAMPIT had done a commendable job which had resulted in the seizure of fake stamp papers worth billions of rupees.

The matter was placed before the State Cabinet by the Chief Minister on December 26. The Cabinet decided to hand over the case to the CBI for further investigation. Roshan Baig resigned from the Cabinet shortly thereafter. Srikumar appeared to be unhappy with the decision to transfer the case to CBI but didn't react in public.

Spread of Naxalism

As Head of Intelligence, matters relating to security were also part of my brief. Those days Maoism, also known as Naxalism, had gained roots in the Western Ghats and this was a cause for concern. On November 17, 2003, I received a report that police had an encounter with Naxals in a village called Idu in Udupi district. The report mentioned that on receipt of information that a group of Naxals was visiting the house of a farmer Ramappa Poojary. Police had surrounded the house and asked the Naxals to surrender. When they didn't follow the instruction, there was an exchange of fire which resulted in the death of two female Naxals - Hajima and Parvati. One woman Yeshoda, a Naxal, had been injured and three had made good their escape. I flew to Mangalore immediately and drove to the place of the incident as it was the first time in the Western Ghat area that an encounter involving Naxals had taken place. I also went to the KMC Hospital in Manipal where the injured Yeshoda had been admitted. I interviewed her about the incident and learnt from her that one of the deceased Hajima hailed from Raichur district. This information unnerved me.

As the former DIG of North-Eastern Range, which covered Raichur district, I was aware that Naxalism had entered our State through Andhra Pradesh and the districts to be affected first were Gulbarga, Raichur and Tumkur, which shared boundary with Andhra Pradesh. A few months earlier, on May 14, Naxals had attacked and tortured a person suspecting him to be a police informant in Pavagada of Tumkur district.

I had learnt that the Naxalite leadership had decided to move away from Raichur and Gulbarga and concentrate on the Western Ghats of the State. This move was consequent to the efforts of Saket Rajan, a former journalism student from Mysore, and an active Naxalite leader. In his report "Social and Economic Conditions of Malnad Area (SOCOMA)" he had argued that the leadership should concentrate on the districts of Shimoga, Udupi and Chikmagalur to spread the ideology. The encounter at Idu had proved this.

Throughout my tenure as ADG, Intelligence, Naxal issue was a major problem that the State had to face. I shall recount more incidents a little later.

5

Dramatic Changes in the State's Political Scenario

On January 21, 2004, when I went to the residence of CM SM Krishna in the morning, he was dressed and ready to go out. After I briefed him about certain important events, he told me that he had to attend a meeting of the Congress members of Parliament from Karnataka in Windsor Manor Hotel, a stone's throw from his residence and left for the meeting. I learnt that the then CM of Maharashtra Vilasrao Deshmukh, AICC General Secretary in-charge of Karnataka, was presiding over this meeting. I waited for the CM at 'Anugraha'.

After about an hour and a half the CM returned from the meeting. By this time Minister DK Shivakumar had arrived at 'Anugraha'. Looking worried, the CM told us that the MPs urged advancement of elections to the State Legislature to coincide with the Parliamentary elections. Prime Minister Atal Bihari Vajpayee had decided to request the Election Commission to advance the elections to the Lok Sabha and thus allow a premature dissolution of the 13th Lok Sabha. What gave him strength was that his party, the BJP, had done well in the assembly elections to four States. He apparently wanted to cash-in on this victory mood and make the country face elections earlier than the scheduled.

The first reaction of Shivakumar was that the CM should not agree for premature assembly polls in Karnataka. By then many more members of legislature arrived at 'Anugraha' and most of them were heard saying that didn't want early elections. T Jayaprakash, IG, Intelligence also came to the CM's residence and he too concurred with the views of others present there.

Later in the day, GS Basavaraj, an MP from Tumkur, met me and disclosed that the CM seemed to be inclined towards the views of the MPs for simultaneous elections, but there was tremendous opposition among the Legislators for this move. Most MLAs wanted elections to be held only in October and didn't want their tenure to be curtailed almost by six months.

On January 28, when I met the CM, he asked my specific opinion about the idea of having simultaneous elections. Minister DK Shivakumar was also present in the room. I told him that whenever simultaneous elections to the State Legislatures and the Parliament were held, the voters tended not to vote candidates belonging to the same political party for both Parliament and the legislature feeling that the national issues are different from the local issues. If an anti-incumbency wave were to operate, his party would not gain much in the legislative elections.

He listened to me intently but by observing his body language I felt that he had already made up his mind. When I came out of the CM's room, Shivakumar, who was standing outside, held a short discussion on this subject with me and stated that he too concurred with my view. I told him to utilize his proximity with Vilasrao Deshmukh and get the decision reversed.

I was later informed that a large number of Congress legislators met the CM and urged him to change this decision. But for reasons I couldn't fathom, the CM remained firm in his decision to go for simultaneous elections. I got a feeling that he was under some pressure to agree for dissolution of the State Legislature. After the decision to go for polls was made, the CM asked me to make an assessment about the outcome of Lok Sabha elections in Karnataka and give him a report.

On February 6th, I learnt that the 13th Lok Sabha was dissolved ahead of its schedule, which meant elections were imminent. Ten days later, on February 16, the CM held a Cabinet meeting wherein it was decided to dissolve the Karnataka Assembly. Soon after the Cabinet meeting, Krishna met the Governor of Karnataka TN Chaturvedi and submitted the letter recommending dissolution of the eleventh Legislative Assembly.

When I met the CM on March 17, I suggested that he should contest from one more constituency, besides his constituency of Maddur just to be on the safer side. I told him about my advice to the then CM R Gundu Rao decades ago to contest from Chitapur apart from his home constituency of Somwarpet. I also pointed out that Sonia Gandhi herself had chosen Bellary apart from Amethi to contest for Lok Sabha. He listened to me patiently but didn't give out his mind. But on March 31, I learnt that he had decided to change his constituency from Maddur in Mandya district to Chamarajpet in Bangalore City. I thought that there might be strong reasons for the CM to choose a new constituency. Having done so much for the development of Bangalore city, he must have been confident that the voters would prefer him. Secondly, Chamarajpet was the constituency represented by his close follower RV Devraj who might have assured the CM of victory. I had then wondered who would be the Congress candidate in Maddur.

By the first week of March, I had extensively travelled throughout Karnataka to feel the pulse of the electorate. I had come to the conclusion that the ruling Congress party might not win more than 15 Lok Sabha seats and 83 Assembly seats. My report, naturally, caused a furore in the party circles. A few days later, I was called by the CM to his chambers. Many of his senior cabinet ministers were present there. I was asked to explain as to how I had come to such a conclusion. At the time of dissolution, the Congress party had 135 legislators and many Independents were supporting the government headed by SM Krishna. The Janata Dal (Secular) was riddled by dissensions among its ranks. The senior ministers had wondered how I had reported that the Congress would lose as many as 50 seats held then. My report, therefore, was not acceptable to them. I tried to explain stating that we had contacted a section of the voters in each constituency and merely reflected the voters' feelings. What was surprising to them was our finding that the party would virtually be wiped out in Tumkur district. The report which caused them shock resulted in disbelief. As I was leaving the CM's room, I overheard someone remark that I was after all a police officer who cannot understand the nuances of politics and the Intelligence report given by me should be consigned to a dustbin. Some were heard laughing over this remark.

The next few weeks, I was very busy with work related to VIP Security as senior leaders belonging to all political parties were descending on the State for electioneering. I personally supervised the security arrangements for the visits of the Prime Minister of India Atal Bihari Vajpayee, and the Congress President Sonia Gandhi.

An unfortunate incident during this period was the death of popular South Indian film star Soundarya. The star, who was a supporter of the Bharatiya Janata Party, had taken off from the Jakkur airfield in a Cessna aircraft on the morning of April 17 and within minutes of its take off the plane had crashed in the GKVK campus next to the airfield killing all the four passengers.

Not in Favour of Congress

The second assessment of elections was sought and we went about our assessment in a meticulous manner. It was quite obvious that the BJP had gained considerable ground in the coastal districts of Karnataka, apart from the districts of Chikmagalur and Shimoga. The JD(S) was very strong in the old Mysore region. The Hyderabad-Karnataka area which was once a bastion of Congress was also slipping from the party's hands. I reported that the situation had not improved much and at the best, the Congress party may win around 94 seats. I stated that while in 15 constituencies no clear prediction can be made, the BJP and the JD(S) parties put together are likely to get 90 seats and 15 seats might go to Independents and smaller parties. When I reported this to the CM, senior ministers Dharam Singh and Mallikarjuna Kharge were also present with him. They appeared to be quite taken aback by this observation of mine. Because at that time the perception among the media persons and the general public was that the Congress party, under the leadership of SM Krishna, had given good governance.

What I hadn't known at that time was that certain individuals close to the CM had commissioned a private agency to conduct a survey throughout the State and the said agency had predicted a landslide victory for the Congress. I was told that the agency, which was a marketing consultancy firm based out of Bangalore, had stated that the Congress party would win 124 seats. Many astrologers, whom I had named as 'Asthana Purohits', had also predicted a clear majority to the party. Therefore, no Congressman took our assessment seriously.

I cannot forget an incident that happened when I was travelling to Delhi. In that aircraft were some senior Congress ministers accompanied by astrologer Dwarakanath. They were travelling in business class. A minister, on noticing me sitting in the front row of economy class, called me to the cabin where the ministers were sitting. They asked me point blank how many seats the Congress party would get in the elections. Without batting an eyelid I said '84'. They all looked at Dwarakanath. He stared at me and told me that I would be proved wrong.

The results were announced on May 13, I was indeed proved wrong. The Congress party had won only 65 seats whereas the BJP had secured 79 seats and had emerged on top. The JD(S) had made impressive gains by getting 58 seats. My only assessment which was proved somewhat right was the victories of Independent candidates. Against my prediction of 15, 13 Independents had emerged victorious. It was a hung assembly for the first time in the history of Karnataka. Everyone had missed reading the mind of the electorate.

Of the 13 seats in Tumkur, the Congress won only one. As expected it won 10 seats in Bangalore returning the CM from Chamarajpet. In the home district of the CM, the Congress won only two seats. In the Maddur constituency which was vacated by SM Krishna, the Congress candidate DC Tammanna won. The JD(S) made significant gains in the Hyderabad-Karnataka area whereas the BJP made a sweep in the coastal region of the State.

My assessment about the Lok Sabha results also had gone wrong. Against my report that the Congress would win 15 seats, it won only 8 and the BJP won 18. As most Congress MLAs had feared right from the beginning, the decision of the party for simultaneous elections to both Lok Sabha and State Legislature had proved very costly.

On May 14, I met the CM in his residence. He was in a sombre mood. I told him how very sorry I was for his party. He said, "You had never given me a rosy picture of the results. You had told me that more than 20 ministers in my cabinet would lose. But it was not possible for us to refuse giving tickets to them." He left for Delhi the same evening.

When he returned to Bangalore three days later, I met him at his residence. He was in a good mood and said that Congress would be forming a government with the help of the JD(S), and if the JD(S) didn't agree for the coalition, President's Rule would become inevitable. He told me that a clear picture would emerge only after the formation of government at the national level.

No single party had obtained the numbers to form a government at the national level and alliances between political parties had become inevitable. Fast-paced political developments took place. The Congress party was able to muster 275 members of Lok Sabha and formed an alliance called the United Progressive Alliance. Dr Manmohan Singh was elected as Prime Minister. Krishna was present in Delhi during this time.

On May 23, the CM returned from Delhi and indicated to me about the formation of a coalition government in Karnataka. On the next day, the JD(S) held a meeting of its legislators at a resort outside Bangalore and I learnt that they had agreed to form the government along with the Congress. On the same day, a meeting of the Congress Legislature Party was held at Vidhana Soudha. The newly elected leaders had authorized the party leadership to pick their leader. When I met SM Krishna in the evening at 'Anugraha', he appeared distraught. Through my sources, I learnt that the person to be chosen as the leader of the Congress Legislature Party (CLP) had to be acceptable to the JD(S) leadership too as the CLP leader would also be the next Chief Minister. Probably because of this, a second meeting of the CLP was held in the evening and Dharam Singh's election as the leader was confirmed at 10 PM. When asked about this, Krishna told me that Dharam Singh was a nice person and would carry everyone along with him.

Some journalist friends later told me that many senior leaders of the Congress were quite upset with the election of Dharam Singh as CLP leader, he was not the first choice of the legislators. He was the choice of Deve Gowda to be the next Chief Minister of Karnataka. It was a sort of political coup.

The next morning I met Dharam Singh at his residence and congratulated him. Both of us had known each other for a very long time. He was very happy and told me that the Congress high command, and especially Pranab Mukherjee, had backed him.

After meeting Singh, I met Krishna. We had coffee together. He was in a reflective mood. I told him that I would miss him and thanked him for all the encouragement he had given me not only as the Chief of Intelligence but also as the Head of the State Information Department. We agreed to keep in touch.

6

SM Krishna – As I Saw Him

During the entire five year tenure of Chief Minister SM Krishna two major problems dogged the State Government. The first was undoubtedly the notorious forest brigand Veerappan. A mention has been made about the tensions Veerappan had caused after he abducted Dr Rajkumar. After the release of the veteran actor in November 2000, it was expected that Veerappan would lie low but that was not to be.

On August 25, 2002, Veerappan kidnapped H Nagappa, a former Karnataka minister in the cabinet of JH Patel, from his residence in Kamagere in Hanur village in Chamarajanagar district. Nagappa, who had been defeated in the Assembly elections in 1999, used to openly criticize Veerappan. The kidnap of the ex-MLA was quite similar to the kidnap of Dr Rajkumar. The only difference was that Nagappa had been provided a gunman by the government.

After the kidnap, the brigand made demands similar to those he had made when he had kept Dr Rajkumar in custody. Though the State Government was not under the same amount of pressure as it had been during the actor's abduction, the kidnapping of an important political personality of the State had exposed the chinks in the State's armour and had caused embarrassment to the government.

The discovery of the bullet-ridden decomposed body of Dr Nagappa in the forests on December 8, 106 days after his kidnap, had pained everyone. Though Veerappan later claimed that he had not been responsible for the politician's death, none believed him. Losing an influential leader to the designs of bandit was definitely a black mark for the government.

The very first week after assuming charge as Chief of Intelligence, I visited most of the areas in Chamarajanagar district which had seen the strikes by the ruthless criminal. This included the residence of Dr Nagappa. After the death of Dr Nagappa, Veerappan appeared to remain quiet, though we did hear that he had close contacts with LTTE and that he was planning to kidnap a Member of Parliament or a foreign national. As the government could ill-afford to ignore any threat by Veerappan, I had instructed my officers to remain ever alert.

The second problem which came to worry the CM constantly was the Cauvery river water dispute with Tamil Nadu. Severe drought had affected most parts of the State year after year and Karnataka could ill afford to release water to its neighbour. In October 2002, the Supreme Court had come down heavily on the Chief Minister Krishna for non-compliance of its order (of releasing Cauvery water to Tamil Nadu) and had even threatened taking up a case of contempt.

Though being under so much of pressures, Krishna had never lost his cool and equanimity.

A Choosy Leader

Having interacted with him almost on a daily basis for nine months, I had come to understand him a little better than what I had known him as the Director of Information. I must mention that any Chief of Intelligence develops a symbiotic relationship with the Chief Minister he serves. This is because of the constant interactions and mutual dependence. Though an officer tries to maintain the relationship as official as possible, an iota of subjectivity does creep in.

Krishna was a very private individual and chose his company. Though I visited his residence every day, I would not get to see any of his family members. Of course, only Mrs Prema Krishna lived in 'Anugraha' and both their daughters had lived elsewhere. Whenever his close family members came to visit them, they would enter the house from the side door and straight proceed to the residential portion on the first floor. I came to see his son-in-law VG Siddartha only months after I became ADG Intelligence.

Krishna didn't like security men hovering around him. We had provided two personal security officers for him from the Police Department and he had developed trust with these two individuals. One of them, R Manjunatha later joined politics, contested assembly elections in 2018 and was elected MLA from Dasarahalli constituency on a JD(S) ticket. Except for those two, who would take care of his immediate personal needs, no one went close to the CM.

The CM was quite fond of giving his security personnel a slip whenever he could. Once he caused me and all others involved in his security great tension by taking a new car for a test drive on the streets of Bangalore. Till he returned home, we spent really anxious moments and on his return, he saw our worried faces and gave a mischievous smile! I learnt later that the CM was very fond of driving and whenever he saw a new car, he wanted to take it for a drive.

It was very difficult for me to keep a track of Krishna's movements especially when he went out of Karnataka. When Gundu Rao was the CM, the SP in-charge of CM's security would travel with the CM wherever he went, but Krishna did not follow this practice. This caused a lot of hardship for us. Whenever we received his tour schedule, we would alert the police officials of the State concerned to provide him security but in the absence of an officer of Karnataka Police being with the CM, security liaison work had become very difficult for us. I remember a police officer of Delhi Police telling me sheepishly that they had 'lost' the car of the CM which they were escorting.

Sometimes the CM would suddenly change his tour schedule and cause a lot of worry to me. He would go to Delhi and instead of returning to Bangalore as per schedule, he would suddenly fly to Mumbai or some other city. We would come to know about this change only if his OSD decided to inform me. The CM would also prefer to stay in The Claridges Hotel in Delhi instead of Karnataka Bhavan. Sometimes he would not go to The Claridges at all but check into some other hotel. This had posed some difficulties for me in communicating certain important messages to the CM. Fortunately the OSD BN Krishnaiah would be available on phone 24×7 and I could communicate important matters through him to the CM.

An Enigma

Certain decisions of Krishna as the Chief Minister still remain an enigma to me. To cite a few, in December 2001, the Department of Information had organized the annual State Film Award presentation function in Bangalore. As Bangalore had missed hosting the IFFI (International Film Festival of India), we wanted to make it a glittering event. When I invited the CM to be the Chief Guest and present the awards, he refused stating that he had some other engagement to attend to. We, therefore, requested the Governor of Karnataka to present the awards. The then Governor VS Rama Devi graciously agreed to attend the function and presented awards.

When the function was underway at the Ambedkar Bhavan in Bangalore, the CM entered the hall along with his wife and sat with the audience. There was a flutter among the audience on seeing him. I was quite surprised by his presence as he had told me that he would not attend. I greeted him and requested him to come on the stage. He didn't oblige us for reasons best known to him. Many award winners were disappointed by his refusal to go on the stage and give away some awards.

Similarly, the sudden decision of the State Government not to host the International Film Festival in Bangalore earlier, citing the drought in the State as the reason had surprised many film personalities.

The government of Karnataka had agreed to organise the 32nd International Film Festival of India in Bangalore from 10th October 2001 onwards. It had been agreed that the cost of organizing the festival (₹5 crore) was to be split between the Union and the State Governments. The 23rd edition of this festival, held in Bangalore in 1992, had been a great success and everyone was eagerly looking forward to its 32nd edition. Department of Information, of whom I was the head, was entrusted with the task of organizing the 32nd IFFI.

My Minister Prof BK Chandrasekhar had directed us that we should strive hard to see that the Festival was a roaring success. He had desired that after the tension-filled 108 days of Dr Rajkumar's abduction, the people of Karnataka should have something exciting to look forward to. I had held several rounds of meetings with the officials of the Directorate of Film Festivals in Delhi in connection with the organization of the Festival.

Several subcommittees were constituted for the smooth organization of the event as we wanted to use the platform of IFFI to globally showcase the garden city of Bangalore and the cultural richness of the State of Karnataka. Veteran film directors like MS Sathyu and BV Karanth had been roped in to give suggestions to make the opening ceremony a memorable event. Malti Sahai, the Director of Film Festivals, made a few visits to Bangalore from Delhi and gave us her valuable suggestions. She indicated that as per protocol the Union Minister for Information and Broadcasting Sushma Swaraj was to be the Chairperson of the Organising Committee and the CM of Karnataka was to be the Co-Chairperson.

When she met the Chief Secretary and the Principal Secretary to the CM along with me, she was told that the CM would not like to be the Co-Chairperson and that he had desired that the Minister in-Charge of Information Department should be the co-chairperson. She appeared disappointed but reluctantly agreed. Meanwhile, a committee headed by veteran film director Shaji Karun had selected the films for the Panorama section and we were happy that four Kannada films had made the grade. Sree Kanteerava Stadium in Bangalore was to be the venue for the opening ceremony.

On June 29, Sushma Swaraj came to Bangalore along with a retinue of officials from Delhi to oversee the preparations for the Festival. She chaired a meeting of those connected with the Festival organisation at the Vidhana Soudha. The film personalities present in the meeting requested her that an eminent person from the Kannada film industry should be given the honour of opening the festival and a Kannada film retrospective should also be screened. She agreed with both the suggestions.

After this meeting concluded, I heard murmurs that the State Government was not happy with the constitution of the Organising Committee of the IFFI as the CM of Karnataka had not been given the honour of chairing the Organising Committee. When I informally broached this topic with the officers of the Union Government, I was told that since the IFFI came under the domain of the Central Government, only the Union Minister could be made the Chairperson of the organizing committee.

On September 18, I was told that the State Government wanted postponement of IFFI in view of the severe drought affecting the State. I rushed to Chief Minister's office and met his Secretary and Principal Secretary to verify the news. Both of them gave me an impression that it was the Central Government which wanted the postponement of IFFI. I was told that this matter was also discussed in the State Cabinet and most senior ministers favoured its postponement.

There was a widespread dissatisfaction not only in the Kannada film industry but also among the general public about this decision. Subsequently, on receipt of a request by the State Government, the Central Government headed by Atal Bihari Vajpayee decided to cancel the 32nd edition of IFFI itself. Probably they had no time to organize the festival elsewhere.

The attack on the World Trade Centre in New York on Septemeber 11 was also given as a reason for cancelling the 32nd IFFI.

What I could not fathom was that the State was reeling under drought even when the decision to hold the IFFI in Bangalore was taken. When considerable time and effort had been spent by many to make the event a grand success, the decision to postpone the Festival, just three weeks prior to the event, was a surprise even to the CM's friends in the film industry.

Krishna did have good friends in the Kannada film industry. His close friend RT Narayan's foster daughter Ramya not only became a famous actress but also was elected to Lok Sabha from the CM's home district of Mandya on a Congress ticket. Another famous Kannada film actor Ambareesh from Mandya was a Minister of State at the Centre and a Minister in the State cabinet.

Former industrialist RT Narayan used to meet the CM along with the CM's other close friends. Narayan, who would always be dressed in a white 'Pyjama-Kurta' maintained a very low profile. I was told that he was from Mysore, unmarried and a graduate in agriculture. A Brahmin by birth, he had lived for some years in Mumbai and had returned to Mysore and had set up an industry.

He and the CM were 'doubles partners' in tennis. He was an office-bearer of Karnataka Lawn Tennis Association and was instrumental in renovating its tennis stadium in Bangalore. He too was credited with getting the ATP World Doubles Challenge Cup Tennis match brought to Bangalore. He had a permanent room in the West End Hotel, Bangalore where I was told he would stay during weekdays. There were rumours that Narayan was part of the 'kitchen cabinet' of Krishna and was instrumental in many of the political and administrative decisions taken by the CM.

Narayan was only a nodding acquaintance to me and we had spoken to each other only once when we both had attended a Carnatic classical music concert. In that short interaction, he had told me that most people whom Krishna had befriended were known to the CM for decades and that Krishna was fond of jokes and would laugh heartily whenever they met. Several years later, Narayan had telephoned me with a request to help his foster daughter ward off a stalker and I had done the needful.

Krishna was very fond of tennis and sometimes would go to the Tennis Association courts in Cubbon Park at Bangalore and play a game or two. He was also elected the President of the Karnataka State Lawn Tennis Association and in that capacity was responsible for the successful ATP World ranking doubles tour held in KSLTA courts in January-February 2002. He would also attend important matches played in Bangalore and watch such matches played outside on television.

He was a voracious reader and spent considerable time reading books. Wherever he travelled, he would take one or two books with him. He would read articles in the Editorial pages of newspapers with interest. Once his assistant had told me that Krishna was allergic to the ink residue found on newspapers and hence before the papers were handed over to the CM, they had to be thoroughly dusted.

Krishna was quite close to several important media persons. He would give special interviews to select journalists. When someone had told me that he had consulted a top PR consultant Dilip Cherian for an image makeover, I had replied to him that without any external help Krishna had built for him an excellent image and no one could give him any lesson in that aspect.

Because of his impressive academic qualifications, Krishna could speak on many subjects authoritatively. After obtaining his BA degree from Maharaja's College, Mysore, he had studied Law at Bangalore and later on had secured his MCL degree from Southern Methodist University in Dallas, USA. I was lucky to have attended a lecture given by him at IIT, Delhi which was very well received. He knew how to market himself and the State of which he was the CM.

The CM was fond of listening to classical Carnatic music. I had seen him attend many music concerts organized annually by the Rama Seva Mandali at Fort High School, Bangalore. When he learnt about my interest in Carnatic classical music I became one of the privileged invitees for a private concert by vocalist Sudha Raghunathan he had organised.

Much had been written about Krishna's excellent dress sense. He would dress for the occasion. He was at ease wearing lounge suits or a 'Pyjama-Kurta' with a dupatta thrown stylishly around his neck. Once when I admired the 'band gala' suit he was wearing and its design, he told me that he had designed the suit himself and explained the intricacies of its design. When I got a similar suit stitched for myself and wore it, he was the first to notice and appreciate.

Ashram Visit

I can recollect only one occasion wherein SM Krishna showed his annoyance towards me. He was invited to be a guest at an ashram in Bidadi near Bangalore city. The Deputy Commissioner of Bangalore Rural district Kani Ram spoke to me and said that it would not be desirable for the CM to visit the ashram as there were some complaints of land encroachment against the ashram. I got a quick enquiry conducted and was told that the pontiff of that ashram who belonged to Tamil Nadu was controversial. When the CM was about to leave his residence for the ashram along with his wife, I stopped him and advised him to cancel the visit. Kani Ram who was also standing there told the CM the same thing. The CM showed great annoyance towards both of us, sat in the car and proceeded towards the ashram. Poor Kani Ram had to follow the CM's car and remain present in the Ashram function attended by the CM. I recall that it was the only time SM Krishna had ever rebuffed me.

I had noticed that the CM was not overtly religious like many politicians. I had not seen any astrologer, Swamiji or godman coming close to the CM. Only once during my tenure with Krishna, I had heard that the pontiff of Pejawara Matha Vishvesha Theertha Swamiji had been invited to visit his home and that the Swamiji had to unavoidably cancel the visit at the last minute. I had seen Krishna used to put *vibhuti* (sacred ash) every morning after his bath.

The CM, I had observed, had a secretive nature. He usually didn't give out his thoughts to any person whom he had not known for a long period of time. He trusted very few officers. One of them was Jayakar Jerome, who was at that time functioning as the Commissioner of Bangalore Development Authority. When Krishna became the Governor of Maharashtra he took Jerome to Mumbai as his Secretary. When Krishna was the External Affairs Minister of Government of India, Jerome was appointed as Ambassador to Slovenia. At that time Jerome had retired from service and many eyebrows had been raised about his appointment.

I had known Jerome since my days as Asst Superintendent of Police in Hospet Sub-Division in 1979. Jerome, an officer of the Karnataka Administrative Service, was the Deputy Administrator of Tungabhadra Command Area Development Agency then. His headquarters was Munirabad, close to Hospet. The Administrator was AS Melkote, IAS. K Jairaj was the then Assistant Commissioner of Hospet revenue Sub-Division and all the four of us used to meet often. Though we went a long way, none of us discussed anything official during our days with SM Krishna. Another officer whom I found to be close to the Chief Minister was IAS officer KN Srivastava who was at that time Chairman of the four Power Transmission Corporations. He was a very low profile officer and never exhibited his proximity to the Chief Minister. Apart from them, I had seen IAS officers Jyotiramalingam and AK Manoli being somewhat close to the CM.

Despite the heavy weight of the crown he wore, Krishna remained calm and composed throughout his tenure as Chief Minister and pursued the interests which were close to his heart. As I took leave of him on May 25, 2004, I wondered what would have happened if he had not agreed to go for assembly elections along with the Lok Sabha polls. Would the history of Karnataka have changed? It is very hard to guess.

7

With Dharam Singh as Chief Minister

On May 26, 2004 the CM designate Dharam Singh left for Delhi. Some of the newly elected MLAs from the Janata Dal (Secular) along with their leaders also left for Delhi. Quick political developments took place on May 27. I was told that there were some issues relating to the post of Deputy Chief Minister, who was to be from the JD(S). Late in the night, Swamy, Dharam Singh's personal assistant spoke to me from Delhi stating that the swearing-in ceremony would be held the next day and Siddaramaiah would be the Deputy Chief Minister.

On his arrival at Bangalore on the 28, I met Singh at Kumara Krupa Guest House and told him that it is the prerogative of the CM to choose his Chief of Intelligence and that it is the usual practice that the previous incumbent is replaced by a new one. I told him that I would be happy to work in whichever post he deems fit to give me. He smiled and said that he had watched me closely when I was working with SM Krishna and that I had done a good job in Intelligence and that I should continue with him too. I profusely thanked him for the confidence he had reposed in me.

He indicated then that he would like to have SV Ranganath, an IAS officer of 1975 batch to be his Principal Secretary and that I should get the files moving for his repatriation to the State from the Central Government service. Ranganath had only recently gone on deputation to Government of India after serving a few years as the Principal Secretary to SM Krishna.

He had served in the secretariat of Chief Ministers, Ramakrishna Hegde, Deve Gowda and Veerappa Moily earlier. In place of Shankaralinge Gowda, Siddaiah, a batch-mate of Gowda came as Secretary-1 to the CM. In place of Jawaid Akhtar, Rakesh Singh joined the CM's office as Secretary-2 to the CM.

The CM had indicated that he would like to continue BN Krishnaiah as his Officer on Special Duty. Krishnaiah had endeared himself to everyone around him. He had a tremendous reservoir of energy and would not get tired working long hours. He had a very sharp mind and hundreds of telephone numbers were literally at his fingertips. I had known that Dharam Singh too had a similar memory for numbers and could recall cell phone numbers of many persons instantly. Krishnaiah would always be smiling and never misused his proximity with the CM. He used to have two mobile phones and an extra battery as he had to be speaking on phone for hours on end. He knew virtually every politician in Karnataka. Because of his impeccable manners, he was liked by everyone. Probably that was the reason why he created a record of sorts by continuously working with four Chief Ministers - SM Krishna, Dharam Singh, Kumaraswamy, and BS Yeddyurappa. After working a decade in the CM's secretariat, Krishnaiah was transferred after he was promoted to the IAS. When HD Kumaraswamy became the CM in 2018, Krishnaiah once again became OSD to CM, though he had retired from the government service. However, he is yet to beat the record of Ranganath of serving six Chief Ministers of Karnataka.

That afternoon the swearing of the CM and Deputy CM took place at Raj Bhavan. The crowds which had gathered at the venue were quite unruly and everyone rushed towards the new CM and Deputy CM to congratulate them. The road outside Raj Bhavan was full of supporters of both political parties and there was a massive traffic jam. I was, however, able to meet the Deputy CM and congratulate him.

First Hurdle

As most political pundits expected the first major hurdle to be crossed by the CM was the expansion of his cabinet. After several rounds of unending meetings both in Bangalore and in Delhi five names each from both the parties were finalized on June 4th. The CM who spoke to me from Delhi revealed the names of the legislators who were selected to be the ministers and asked me to communicate the news to the concerned and request them to be ready for the swearing-in ceremony.

Mallikarjuna Kharge, PGR Sindhia, MP Prakash, D Manjunath, Prakash Hukkeri, SR More, HD Revanna, Mirajuddin Patil and Tanveer Sait were the ministers who were sworn in on June 5. Non-inclusion of senior Congressmen RV Deshpande, HK Patil, and DK Shivakumar in the new cabinet surprised many political observers. Knowing the animosity between Deve Gowda and Shivakumar, I was not surprised about Kumar's exclusion but thought that this would pose problems to the coalition government in the future. The Chief Minister gave a statement that the cabinet would be further expanded soon in order to keep the hopes alive in the minds of the ministerial aspirants.

The allotment of portfolios posed the next big challenge and the difficulties of running a coalition government was soon evident to me and I wondered whether I would be able to function effectively in the coalition set up.

On June 7, I was summoned to the West End Hotel by Deve Gowda's son HD Kumaraswamy. Former Minister S Ramesh of the Congress party was with him. Kumaraswamy said that the government would like me to be the next Commissioner of Police of Bangalore. Surprisingly, the CM, who held the portfolio of home and Intelligence departments, had only recently asked me to continue as Head of Intelligence. I, therefore, surmised that as a member of the Gowda family, Kumaraswamy would be having a strong say in the running of the coalition government in future.

I told Kumaraswamy that as a true public servant, I would go wherever I was posted. He replied that there was a discussion about me by both the parties and that while the JD(S) would have no objection for my continuation in the Intelligence Wing, it wanted a change of IG Intelligence. He asked me to give him some names to replace T Jayaprakash. It was not difficult to guess that the JD(S) leaders, who didn't like SM Krishna, didn't want any officer close to the ex-CM in the Intelligence Wing.

In the meanwhile, many of the new ministers were not happy with the portfolios allotted to them and were pressuring the CM for giving them better departments. The CM was also worried about the release of Cauvery river water to Tamil Nadu. The Prime Minister, Dr Manmohan Singh had telephonically spoken to the Chief Minister and had asked him to release the Cauvery water to Tamil Nadu and the CM had to accede to the request. But he was worried whether the release would result in a protest by the farmers of the State. He had to tread very cautiously. Fortunately, due to copious rains in the catchment area, there were no protests over the release of water to Tamil Nadu.

Very soon, the IGP Intelligence T Jayaprakash was transferred and in his place was posted JV Gaonkar.

Relief for CM

The first political test for Singh came when the elections to the Rajya Sabha from the Legislative Assembly constituency were held in late June. The Congress had decided to field two candidates, namely, the then Union Minister Oscar Fernandes and All India Congress Committee General Secretary, BK Hariprasad. Each candidate was required to get 44 votes. With its available strength in the Assembly, Fernandes could easily get elected. But for the election of Hariprasad, the party had to depend on its ally. Hectic meetings took place in the residence of the CM to develop a strategy to win the second seat. With the support of the alliance partner and independents,

Hariprasad was declared elected. He secured the highest number of 48 votes, surpassing Fernandes, who got 46 votes. There was a triumphant smile on the CM's face when the results were declared.

Another important test for the new CM was the appointment of the new DG and IGP as the incumbent Madiyal was to retire on June 30. Having earlier worked as the Home Minister, Dharam Singh knew all the senior police officers quite well. The seniormost IPS officer at that time was MD Singh but he had only one month to go for his superannuation. Every police officer was curious to know what the CM would do - whether go by seniority or choose a person who had more length of service. When the Chief Minister sought my opinion, I told him that MD Singh was a very honest and upright officer and denying him the post of HOD would be unjust. I firmly believed that every IPS officer aspired to become the Head of the Police Department even for a day and when he was about to get his due, he should not be denied his right. Little did I know then that when my chance to become Head of Police Force came only seven years later, I would be sidelined because I had only six months of service left.

When MD Singh was chosen as the Head of Police Department, some wags in the department were heard commenting that because MD Singh was a Rajput like Dharam Singh, he had been chosen. I thought that this was most unfair to MD Singh, who was not only a very good officer but a very fine sportsman.

Embarrassment from a Cop

The first politically sensitive matter that the CM had to face, however came in the form of a statement by a former Police Officer Sangram Singh. Sangram Singh, a retired Asst Commissioner of Police, had been arrested by the CBI in the Telgi stamp paper scam. When he was produced in a court in Bangalore on July 8, he told the court that he was being made a 'scapegoat' by former Karnataka Chief Minister SM Krishna, the then Home Minister Kharge, former minister DK Shivakumar and Congress leader Ghulam Nabi Azad to 'protect Roshan Baig'. Sangram Singh also stated that he had handed over ₹ 20 crore to a Tamil Nadu actor in connection with the release of matinee idol Dr Rajkumar from the clutches of Veerappan. This was quite explosive indeed.

It has been mentioned in the earlier paragraphs that Roshan Baig, who was a minister in the cabinet of SM Krishna, had resigned in December 2003, after his brother Dr Rehan Baig had surrendered before the STAMPIT team which was investigating the fake stamp paper scam. There were rumours about the involvement of Roshan Baig too in the scam. The CBI, which investigated the case later, gave a clean chit to Roshan Baig and all rumours were set to rest. Dr Rehan Baig was also acquitted by the trial court of all charges against him which was later upheld by the High Court of Karnataka.

The CM was naturally quite upset by the statement by the former police officer. When I went to see him off at the airport on July 9, he advised me to meet Kharge and tell him that he (CM) was in no way connected with Sangram Singh's outburst.

I had very cordial relations with Kharge whom I had first met as an IPS probationer in Gulbarga way back in 1978. Both Dharam Singh and Kharge had become ministers in the cabinet of R Gundu Rao in 1980. As a Minister, Kharge was senior to Dharam Singh. Both were elected from the same district and were very good friends and their political careers in the Congress party had run parallel. Both of them had adorned the post of Home Minister earlier.

I met Kharge at his residence and conveyed the Chief Minister's feelings. Kharge, who appeared visibly upset by Sangram Singh's statement, asked me whether I knew that Sangram Singh was a close relative of the CM. I replied stating that though I was a senior police officer in Karnataka, I didn't know much about Sangram Singh as he hadn't worked with me.

Kharge felt that the statement of Sangram Singh was politically motivated. I tried to convince Kharge that the former police officer might be acting on his own and to escape the clutches of the law might have taken the names of senior politicians in the court. When the CM came back to Bangalore I told him about the outcome of my meeting with Kharge. He immediately summoned top officials and we discussed the problem at hand. While waiting for this meeting, I was told by someone that Sangram Singh was indeed related to the CM and hence the discomfiture of the CM.

As I was returning home, Kharge telephoned me and told me that Sangram Singh's wife and daughter had given an interview to *Star News* reiterating what the former police officer had already told the magistrate. He was extremely upset over this development. To rub salt on the wound, the BJP leader LK Advani who arrived in Bangalore a few days later used Sangram Singh's statement to attack the government.

The CM later gave a statement to the media denying the allegations of Sangram Singh. Not to be outdone, Padma Sangram Singh held a press meet and countered the CM. Before the situation could go out of control, a lot of efforts were made for damage control. But this incident caused some scar in the relationship the CM had with SM Krishna and Kharge.

With fresh problems like admission policy to professional colleges in the State cropping up, the Sangram Singh episode was quickly forgotten.

A short session of the Karnataka Legislature was soon convened and thanks to the diplomatic handling of sensitive issues, Dharam Singh did not have to face any serious problem.

Daily Briefing

Dharam Singh gave more time for my daily briefings. He would not see any visitor at least till 8 AM and I would usually spend an hour with him before that. While Krishna would meet me in his office room after getting ready for the day's work, Singh preferred to talk to me in the balcony of his bedroom. He would be reading the day's newspapers sipping a cup of tea. He would do some yoga exercises after his tea and after my briefing, he would ask me to remain with him for some more time.

If the legislature session was on the late Hanumanta Rao, a very trusted aide of Singh, would be present along with me during my morning briefing of the CM. We would go over the various starred questions and other matters that were listed for the day and prepare the response of the government.

Apart from the CM and his wife, his two sons Vijay Singh and Dr Ajay Singh were staying in 'Anugraha'. While Vijay Singh, who at that time was running an industrial set-up, was married and was having kids, Dr Ajay Singh was yet to be married. All the family members had been introduced to me by the CM and they had been asked to treat me as a member of the family.

On many days, Dharam Singh would ask me to remain present when he met important visitors. As none of his secretarial staff would be present at that time in the morning, he would ask me to note down the points discussed with important visitors and communicate the same to his OSD or the Secretary later. Because this would involve my presence in his residence till 9 AM, he would insist that I have breakfast with him. Prabhavathi Dharam Singh used to personally serve food to the CM. She knew his likes and dislikes and knew what was good for him. Dharam Singh was a frugal eater and usually had some fruits and upma for his breakfast. His family members would partake their breakfast much later.

In the early days of the coalition government, Deve Gowda would call the CM many times and give several directions. I would find HD Revanna, Deve Gowda's son and the PWD Minister, frequently come to 'Anugraha' early in the morning with one or the other request. HD Kumaraswamy, MLA, and the other son of Deve Gowda, would always come with a group of legislators and draw the CM's attention to several problems. His group usually consisted of MLAs N Cheluvaraya Swamy, Zameer Ahmed Khan, HC Balakrishna and Bhoje Gowda. Everyone felt that these four politicians were very close to each other. Each person would bring one or two requests related to transfers of officials or sanction of funds for some government projects in their constituency. I felt that during the first three months, the CM spent more time with JD(S) legislators than his own party men. When I mentioned this to him, he gave a disarming smile.

Singh would also see people from his home district of Gulbarga for whom he had a special fondness. I would always admire Singh's remarkable memory of remembering names. He would talk to each of his Gulbarga visitors by addressing him or her by name. He would also ensure that most persons from his constituency were provided tea and snacks whenever they visited the CM's residence. Sometimes when he would be busy, he would ask his son Dr Ajay Singh or else his aide Swamy to take care of Gulbarga visitors.

Former Minister HC Srikantaiah would also come to 'Anugraha' very often and many times would engage me in conversation while waiting for the CM. Another visitor would be Dasegowda of Shimoga district. In the later days, the MLA of Manvi, NS Bose Raju used to visit 'Anugraha' very regularly. In comparison, SM Krishna would rarely meet a visitor before his breakfast.

Because of my ready availability, Dharam Singh would summon me very often to his office. Sometimes I would spend more than five hours every day in the CM's office. I would get to meet a large number of persons and get to know firsthand what was happening in many parts of the State. This way, I would gather Intelligence first hand.

I must mention here the particular problem I had to face as the Intelligence Chief of a coalition government. My seniors in the department had told me that I was answerable only to the minister who was in-charge of the Intelligence set up, namely the CM himself. But as half the work in the Intelligence is related to law and order and its maintenance, the Home Minister would also like to have inputs from the Head of Intelligence. When I was working with SM Krishna, the then Home Minister Kharge, had made it clear to me that I should brief him on all matters which had a bearing on law and order. Therefore, I used to brief him whenever an important issue like the 'Datta Peetha' problem had cropped up.

An Embarrassing Situation

While working with Dharam Singh, the problem was different. As he was also holding charge of the Home Department, I had only one master. But the Deputy CM Siddaramaiah also wanted inputs, not only relating to law and order but also some political issues. I politely told the Deputy CM that I was not obliged to brief him on such matters and he graciously agreed with me.

A few days after he took charge, the matter of appointment of a Secretary to Finance Department cropped up. Dharam Singh had an officer in mind and told me to talk to Siddaramaiah and get his concurrence for the posting. When I met him in his residence, Siddaramaiah was relaxing on an easy chair and some of his followers were sitting with him. When I approached him and told him that I would like to discuss an important issue, he asked me to mention it in the presence of everyone. I felt embarrassed but had no choice.

The Deputy CM didn't also offer me a seat. When I told the officer's name, he sarcastically remarked that I was suggesting the officer's name because he belonged to my caste. I was startled. I told him that I was bringing a message from the CM and if he (Deputy CM) didn't like the officer, he may refuse to accept the officer, but refrain from talking about my caste. I told him that as a police officer, Khaki is my caste. He mumbled something and dismissed me. From that day onwards I started maintaining a distance as far as possible from the Deputy CM and met him only if my official duties required meeting him.

Over the next few months, I found Siddaramaiah to be quite gentle and his outward appearance was only a façade. I thought I had misjudged him after my first meeting with him. I used to go for my morning walks with him whenever we both stayed in Karnataka Bhavan in Delhi. Our long walks in Nehru Garden made us understand each other better. Except for seeking information about the impending transfers in the police department, he would not seek any other information. I was aware that within his own party he was kept at a distance and he concentrated on his portfolio - Department of Finance.

The post of DG and IGP was falling vacant on the afternoon of July 31 consequent to the retirement of MD Singh. The selection committee recommended three names, SN Borkar of 1968 batch of IPS, and YS Rao and BNP Albuquerque of the 1969 batch. The selection committee left the final decision to the CM. Though many in the department had felt Borkar to be too easy going, the CM once again played safe and went by the formula of seniority. He knew Borkar personally as he came from a family of Congressmen from Uttara Kannada district.

Along with the posting of Borkar, several other changes had to be made among the senior IPS officers. BS Sial, an IPS officer of the 1971 batch had returned to the State after a long tenure with the Union Government. He was hopeful of heading the State CID as the DGP on his promotion, but he was posted as DGP of Prisons. KR Srinivasan, who was Addl DGP, and one year junior to Sial in service, was asked to hold concurrent charge as CID chief. I was told by a colleague that Sial suspected my hand in his not being posted to CID as he had perceived me to be very close to Srinivasan. When I called on Sial on August 6th, he accused me of influencing the CM in his not getting the 'important' post of the Chief of CID. Though I vehemently denied that I had any role to play in the matter, he appeared unconvinced.

8

Arrest of Uma Bharti

From the third week of August 2004, the pending criminal case against Uma Bharti took the centre stage in the State politics. Uma Bharti, the then Chief Minister of the BJP ruled Madhya Pradesh, was an accused in a criminal case registered in Hubli way back in 1994. This was regarding the dispute about hoisting the national tricolour in the 1.5-acre plot of land called Idgah Maidan at the heart of the commercial city of Hubli. This vacant piece of land belonged to Hubli Municipality and had been leased to a Muslim organisation called Anjuman Islam to hold prayers during important festivals. When the Anjuman Islam began constructing some shops at one corner of the land in 1960, a dispute arose and courts had ordered demolition of the shops. The matter was taken to the Supreme Court. Meanwhile, the Sangh Parivar jumped into the fray and claimed that Anjuman had no rights to claim the property which was meant for the public use.

In 1992, when the then BJP President Murali Manohar Joshi, decided to hoist the national flag in Srinagar on the Republic Day after a successful 'Rath Yatra', the party's workers at Hubli wanted to hoist the National flag in the Idgah Maidan simultaneously. It was objected to by local Muslim leaders, and the police prevented the BJP workers from hoisting the flag on January 26. The local leaders were determined to hoist the flag in the Maidan and formed an organization called the 'Rashtradhwaja Gourava Samrakshana Samiti' (Committee to protect the honour of the national flag).

On August 15, 1992, an attempt was once again made to hoist the national flag at the Maidan and again it was thwarted. From then onwards, on every Republic Day and Independence Day, a huge posse of police would be posted at the Maidan two to three days earlier, entry to the Maidan restricted, and the prohibitory orders would be imposed in Hubli to prevent any untoward incident.

The BJP took up this emotive issue for political gains which succeeded in polarising the two major communities. As Hubli would virtually turn a fortress during the Republic and Independence Days, the commercial city suffered a lot due to the flight of business from there. The tough posture by the police, often drafted from other cities and districts, towards the citizenry, caused a serious rift between the police and the public. The matter which gained international prominence became a thorn in the flesh for the government of the day and none had a clue as to how the problem would be resolved.

On August 15, 1994, the BJP leader Uma Bharti, along with several other leaders, led a march towards the Idgah Maidan to hoist the national flag. The police prevented them from entering the Maidan. The group then proceeded towards a nearby locality - Deshpande Nagar. Bharti and others reportedly made fiery speeches which resulted in the crowd becoming unruly and resort to violence. To prevent damages to the public property, the police party at the spot opened fire on the mob, resulting in the death of five persons. The police firing resulted in further deterioration of law and order and it took quite a while to bring the situation under control. In connection with the incidents on that day, cases were registered against Bharti and others. And after investigation, a chargesheet had been filed in the court.

It may not be out of place to digress a little here. Consequent to the Karnataka Assembly elections at the end of 1994, a new government headed by Deve Gowda had come into power and it decided to sort out the Idgah Maidan issue once and for all. On January 26, 1995, the government persuaded

Anjuman Islam, the organisation administering the Idgah Maidan, to hoist the national flag and with this act, the problem saw an end. I was appointed Police Commissioner of the twin cities of Hubli-Dharwad immediately thereafter and under my supervision, the flag was hoisted in the Maidan the second time on August 15, 1995. PGR Sindhia was the Home Minister then.

On receipt of the chargesheet, the court at Hubli issued summons to Bharti and other accused to appear before it. She successfully evaded appearing before the court for years. In 2002, the then government decided to withdraw the case against and notified the court accordingly. But in July 2003, the court did not permit withdrawal of the case citing that certain offences alleged against Bharti and others were exclusively triable by the Sessions Court and hence it had no jurisdiction to permit the withdrawal. Hence the court continued issuing summons to Bharti to appear before it and when she didn't appear started issuing warrants. Even after the issue of non-bailable warrants more than twenty times, Bharti didn't appear before the court. Exasperated, the court issued a non-bailable warrant of arrest once again in July 2004 and directed the DG and IGP of Karnataka to execute the same and produce the accused before the court.

By that time as Bharti had become the Chief Minister of Madhya Pradesh, the then DG and IGP Borkar sought directions from Dharam Singh. Fully knowing that arrest of a CM of another State and bringing her to a court was a ticklish issue, a number of legal luminaries in Bangalore and Delhi were consulted. Everyone was unanimous in giving the opinion that Bharti should be arrested and produced before the court. Otherwise, the DG and IGP would end up in prison for committing contempt of court.

Dharam Singh decided to bring the matter to the notice of his party bosses in Delhi and seek their guidance. I was also asked to go with him to Delhi and explain to the party leaders the legal issues involved. The CM met Suresh Pachauri and Kapil Sibal and sought their inputs. Everyone felt that there was no option left to us except to execute the warrant issued by the court against Bharti.

Borkar and other top police officers were in a dilemma. It was not a joke for a police officer from distant Karnataka to go to Bhopal, arrest the Chief Minister, that too a woman, and bring her safely to the court at Hubli. They feared that the supporters of the CM would prevent the police officers from Karnataka in arresting their CM. The question in the minds of many senior officers was what should be done if such a thing happened. No one had an answer. A series of meetings were held and it was decided that a woman IPS officer D Roopa, who was then Superintendent of Police, Dharwad district, would be sent to Bhopal and she could bring Bharti with her to the court.

On August 22, I had accompanied the CM to Delhi to give him inputs needed to discuss the Uma Bharti case. Dharam Singh also wanted to utilise this opportunity to discuss his cabinet expansion with the Congress high command. Kumaraswamy had also arrived in Delhi and several rounds of talks were held.

On August 23, there was a dramatic development. Bharti resigned as the CM of Madhya Pradesh and handed over charge to Babulal Gaur. She had decided to travel to Hubli by train and present herself before the court. She boarded the train on the August 24 afternoon at Bhopal. Meanwhile, Roopa had arrived in Mumbai and was to take her flight to Bhopal. Knowing about Bharti's departure from Bhopal, Roopa was directed to return to Dharwad and await further instructions.

On the same day, we all returned to Bangalore from Delhi. I was told to proceed immediately to Hubli and watch further developments and keep the government informed. Borkar was asked to personally take care of any law and order situation in Hubli. He was told not to arrest Bharti and allow her to present herself in the court. He also left by road along with Subhash Bharani ADG, Law and Order. We were told that Bharti would not seek bail and would rather go to jail.

At Hubli, on the morning of August 25, the DG and IGP called a meeting of senior officers at Hotel Naveen. Roopa was also present at the meeting. She was asked to board the train about two to three stations prior to Hubli and to apprehend Bharti. I was surprised over this move by the DG and IGP as the government had decided to allow Bharti to present herself before the court. I reminded the DG and IGP about this decision of the government, but he stated that when a warrant of arrest had been issued by a court, and when the entire State was aware of the presence of the accused on the soil of Karnataka, not arresting her and producing her before the court would amount to contempt of court.

While Borkar definitely had a point, I was worried about the repercussions that would ensue. I thought that arresting Bharti, while she was in the train, might enrage a large number of her supporters and might lead to riots in parts of the State where the BJP was strong. I pointed this fact out to the DG and IGP and the other senior officers and they told me that they would deal with the problem if it arose.

By then, the train had already left Belgaum Railway station, where a large number of BJP supporters had greeted Bharti and boarded the same train. I pointed out to the DG and IGP that arresting her while she was travelling in the train might give to a situation if her supporters physically prevented Roopa and others from going anywhere near Bharti. I also reminded the DG and IGP about the instructions of the CM and asked him to speak to the CM. By then Roopa had already boarded the train and had gone into the compartment where the ex-CM of Madhya Pradesh was travelling.

There are many versions of what actually happened in the train compartment of Bharti when the police got into it at Alnavar Railway Station. One version is that Roopa did arrest Bharti and asked her to detrain and come with the police on a road journey to Hubli, and that Bharti refused to comply. When the train started chugging ahead, the police party was forced to travel in the same train. Another version is that no formal arrest was ever made. But what is a fact is that when the train arrived at Hubli Railway Station around 9 AM, where I was present, Bharti emerged out of her compartment as any other passenger would and waved at the crowd holding a huge national flag in her hand. There were thousands of her supporters at the station platform and shouts of 'Bharat Mata Ki Jai' rent the air. As she got down, Ananth Kumar, the State BJP President, is said to have informed the police that she would be going to a Kalyana Mantap where her 'guru', the Swamiji of Pejawar Mutt was staying. After meeting the Swamiji, she performed her *pooja*.

Surrender

Around noon, she came to the court and surrendered. As she didn't seek bail she was remanded to judicial custody for a period of fourteen days. She was taken in a convoy to the Sub-Jail in Hubli but on reaching the jail, the police party was informed that it cannot provide adequate security to the high profile prisoner as it was only a sub jail and was told to take her to Hindalga Prison in Belgaum. Meanwhile the State BJP unit called for a State-wide bundh for the next day.

I decided to follow Bharti's convoy up to Belgaum. As we reached Dharwad, I found to my surprise the convoy going inside the Agricultural University campus. Bharti was taken to the University Guest House by the police who told me that as Bharti wanted to have her prayers and lunch, she was taken there. Within minutes a major drama unfolded.

I was told Bharti refused to move out of the Guest House and wanted to stay there instead of going to jail. What I had not known at that time was that her counsel Dorai Raju had pleaded before the court at Hubli that one of the Inspection Bungalows in the district be converted as a jail to house her and that the court had replied that it had no powers to do so. No one had anticipated such a move by Bharti or her party. The police had only two options - either to get the Agriculture University Guest House declared as a prison, or forcibly take

Bharti to Hindalga Jail in Belgaum. The police officers present wanted the government to take a decision in this regard.

I spoke to the CM, the Chief Secretary, and the Home Secretary and apprised them of the situation. The CM asked me to talk to Bharti and find out from her first hand. Within minutes I was in her room. She was sitting cross-legged on the floor on a mat. I introduced myself and sat on the floor facing her. She expressed surprise at my action and asked how a senior IPS officer like me could sit on the floor. I told her that when a former Chief Minister could sit on the floor, a serving officer could also do likewise. She smiled. I asked her why she was insisting on staying at the Guest House. She replied that she cannot stand the prison smell and also the mosquito menace in prisons. I smiled at her and pointed out that even the guest house where she was present, there were lots of mosquitoes. In jail, I said, she would be provided with a mosquito net or a repellent. She stuck to her guns. I tried hard to make her change her mind but was unsuccessful. I left her room. No officer present there knew what was to be done next.

Meanwhile, BS Yeddyurappa and HN Ananth Kumar who were standing outside accosted me and asked me to somehow convince the CM to declare the guest house as a jail. I asked them to speak to the CM as they had his number. They said they were unable to get the CM on their phone. A few minutes later, I spoke to the Home Secretary Brahm Dutt and explained the situation. He asked me to find out the opinion of the DG and IGP. I tried to look for Borkar or Subhash Bharani but they were not at the spot. The Home Secretary told me that he would call me after speaking to the CM.

Half an hour later, Brahm Dutt called me and asked me to speak to the CM who was sitting next to him. I explained the situation to the CM and told him that there were only two options before him - agree to the request, or forcibly take Bharti to Hindalga Jail. I opined that forcibly taking her might result in a serious law and order situation. I reminded him that the BJP had already called for Karnataka Bundh for the next day. The CM listened to me patiently and told me that he would talk to Yeddyurappa after a few minutes. Soon the CM called me on my cell phone and asked me to pass on my handset to Yeddyurappa. He spoke with both Yeddyurappa and Ananth Kumar at length.

Brahm Dutt once again called me and informed me that the government had decided to declare the Agriculture University Guest House as a temporary prison and told me to be in touch with the Deputy Commissioner of Dharwad district. I explained the situation to the DC. Within an hour he met me at the Guest House with a Fax copy of the Government Order declaring the Agriculture University Guest House at Dharwad as a prison. It must be stated here that there was nothing unusual in declaring any place as a prison and take it under the government's control. During the agitation for Datta Peetha in Chikmagalur only a few years ago, a school had been declared as a prison and a number of agitators had been imprisoned there.

With the State Government dropping the charges against her, Bharti was released from jail. Four days later she set off on her 'Tiranga Yatra' from Hubli to Jallianwala Bagh. The Yatra commenced from Rani Chennamma Circle at Hubli, literally a stone's throw from the Idgah Maidan and was flagged off by LK Advani.

It may not be out of place if a mention is made that Dharam Singh had close contacts with many politicians from Madhya Pradesh. The then Union HRD Minister Arjun Singh was quite close to him. When Arjun Singh visited Bangalore, the CM had hosted a dinner for him at his residence. The CM's daughter-in-law Sonal Singh's grandfather was SS Sisodia from Ujjain was the Minister of State for Finance in the Union Cabinet. He was also in the co-operative movement.

Sweet Victory

On August 28, Dharam Singh completed three months in office. Except the problems regarding admissions to professional colleges through a common entrance test no other serious issue had cropped up. I was, however, worried about the rising Naxal menace in the Western Ghats. There were minor skirmishes between the Naxals and the police sporadically in Chikmagalur district. On October 7, one police Head Constable was reportedly kidnapped by Naxals in Mogebayalu near Sringeri but was later released. This resulted in an increased police operation against Naxals.

Meanwhile, the CM had to concentrate on the impending Bidar Lok Sabha constituency bye-election which had been necessitated due to the demise of the 96-year-old BJP leader Ramachandra Veerappa, in late July. Veerappa, a dalit leader, was a veteran politician and had won the Lok Sabha seat for six times. He was an affable gentleman who was liked by all. He had imbibed the Gandhian principles. I had a good rapport with him while I was serving as Superintendent of Police of Bidar district and DIG of the Gulbarga Range.

As Dharam Singh belonged to the Hyderabad-Karnataka area, the party high command expected him to get the Congress party win the bye-election. The first problem faced by the party was to find a suitable candidate. Normally in such bye-election, as 'sympathy factor' plays a role, voters tend to elect a candidate who is related to the departed leader or the one who belongs to the party represented by him. The Congress party settled for a former MP Narasingharao Suryavamshi as the party candidate. But very unexpectedly, the alliance partner JD(S) thwarted the plans of Congress by fielding Babu Honna Naik as its candidate. BJP fielded Basavaraj Arya, the son of Veerappa assuming that he would be able to garner sympathy votes. All the three parties campaigned vigorously. The CM wanted me to make a quick assessment of the situation. I told him that Suryavamshi might in all probability win, but it would happen if the CM himself actively campaigned in the district.

Dharam Singh took this election as a prestige issue and campaigned hard. What became worrisome to him later was the statement by Deve Gowda that if his party candidate lost, there would be President's Rule in the State. The voting was held on October 13 and the voter turn-out was quite poor. Everyone kept their fingers crossed.

When the results began trickling on October 16, I was at 'Anugraha' glued to TV along with the CM. After the first four rounds of counting the Congress candidate Suryavamshi had emerged at the top. He continued to maintain the lead and won by a margin of over 14,000 votes. Dharam Singh could not hide his joy. Even before the final results were out, he spoke to Sonia Gandhi and informed her about the victory. He told me that he had suspected that some of his party leaders had worked to sabotage the chances of the party candidate. This was apparently done to get him a bad name. When I expressed fears about the threat by the JD(S) supremo of President's Rule, he said that he would be going to Delhi soon and with the cabinet expansion things would iron out.

Dharam Singh left for Delhi on October 17, and camped there. He called me to say that he would finalise the names of his new ministers and also finalise the names of candidates for the elections to the Legislative Council. Around the midnight of October 18, when I received a call from CM's OSD Krishnaiah from Delhi I picked up my phone with a lot of trepidation. The officer asked me whether it is true that forest brigand Veerappan was killed. I told him that though I had heard rumours to that effect, without getting an official confirmation, I would not venture to confirm or deny the rumour and disconnected the phone. I immediately called the ADG, Intelligence of Tamil Nadu, Venkatakrishna who confirmed that Veerappan indeed had been killed in an encounter with the Tamil Nadu STF only a few hours ago. I called the CM on his mobile phone and informed him. Like all of us he was overjoyed.

On October 21, the CM attended the police commemoration day parade at Bangalore and soon after decided to leave for Mangalore. He suddenly asked me to accompany him on his tour and I travelled in his helicopter in my ceremonial uniform. When he attended some functions in Mangalore, I held a review meeting of anti-Naxal operations in the office of the IGP, Western Range. The return copter ride on the Western Ghats was very scary indeed. We flew very low and the pilot had to manoeuvre the helicopter crisscrossing various peaks. The ride was quite bumpy. I had earlier flown in the helicopters which were escorting the Prime Minister of India. They were sturdy two engine Russian helicopters and the copter in which I was flying was a single engine Chetak copter. The past crashing of helicopters carrying VIPs came to my mind. Thankfully we landed safely in Bangalore.

Within days, another problem arose. The leaders of the JD(S) did not want DK Shivakumar to be inducted into the cabinet and this gave rise to protests by some Congress leaders. They were vociferous in mentioning that the alliance partner cannot dictate as to who should be made ministers by the Congress party.

On October 27, I got a call from my friend and colleague K Vijay Kumar, ADG of Tamil Nadu STF, that he was in Bangalore and that he would like to meet the CM. We had a breakfast meeting with him in 'Anugraha' attended by the Deputy CM Siddaramaiah. Later on, we requested him to address the media about how Veerappan was killed by STF in the encounter held 10 days ago. A hasty press meet was organised at the home office of the CM where Vijay Kumar detailed how they were able to trap Veerappan and his associates and ultimately kill them when they refused to surrender.

The killing of Veerappan by Tamil Nadu STF did come as a damper to Karnataka Police who had worked very hard over the years to decimate the brigand's gang to less than ten. Karnataka STF deserved appreciation for the excellent work they had done over the years.

The CM of Tamil Nadu Jayalalithaa had announced handsome rewards to the police officials of Tamil Nadu who were part of Veerappan operations which included providing a free house site. We soon had a similar demand from the officers and men who were part of Karnataka STF. Shankar Bidari, who had led the STF for a long period was vociferous in the demand that Karnataka must recognise the hard work put in by STF personnel over so many years and show a similar gesture as Tamil Nadu.

While giving suitable cash rewards to the STF personnel didn't pose a problem to the State, there were simply not enough house sites available in Bangalore to be distributed to the eligible personnel. How exactly would one determine the relative contribution of each member of the STF became a subject matter of innumerable meetings at various levels of the government and at last a formula was hammered out.

As expected, it was not satisfactory to all the stakeholders. Even after presenting cash rewards to the concerned personnel in July 2006, there were murmurs of dissent.

9

Datta Jayanti Celebrations and Threat from Naxals

By the end of October 2004, I sensed that all was not well between the two coalition partners. The government had been formed almost six months ago and both the parties were not very comfortable with each other.

On November 27, in a surprise move, SM Krishna was appointed the Governor of Maharashtra. I remarked to the CM that probably his coalition partners would be happy that the senior Congress leader would be away from Karnataka politics. I told him that Deve Gowda had been planning to write a letter to the Prime Minister Dr Manmohan Singh about some irregularities in the Bangalore Development Authority. The former PM had earlier, in August 2004, written a letter to the CM containing an allegation of corruption in matters related to BDA and that the former CM SM Krishna had rubbished this letter as an attempt to tarnish the image of the Congress party.

I told the CM that as Krishna would be vacating his seat as Member of Chamarajpet Legislative Assembly, he should also concentrate on the bye-election. We both thought that RV Devraj, a close confidant of SM Krishna and former MLA of the same constituency would be the inevitable candidate from the Congress party.

Though Dharam Singh had cordial relations with Deve Gowda, because of his preoccupation with official duties, he could not meet Deve Gowda very often. Kumaraswamy was meeting the CM more often. But the real channel of communication between the CM and the former PM was KK Murthy.

KK Murthy was the Chairman of the Bangalore Development Authority when Gundu Rao was the Chief Minister. He, as the Chairman of Academy of Music, was instrumental in getting the violin shaped auditorium, Chowdaiah Memorial Hall, constructed in Bangalore. He was very close both to Mallikarjuna Kharge and Dharam Singh. I was aware that all the three friends used to meet regularly. I was also aware that he wanted to contest on Congress ticket the assembly elections from Holalkere constituency in Chitradurga district once. Many journalists had told me that he was one of the persons responsible for helping the Congress and the JD(S) form a coalition government. Murthy would always be dressed in a safari suit.

On the morning of November 28, I met the CM and told him that I had learnt of a plan by the BJP to destabilise his government by having a truck with the JD(S). The CM did not believe me and said that such a situation was not possible. He spoke to KK Murthy and even Murthy had no clue about such possible development. The CM later spoke to Deve Gowda himself. I am unaware as to what transpired between the two. What I know is that on November 29 Dharam Singh told me that he would go to Delhi very soon and finalise the cabinet expansion. In hindsight, I now feel that the BJP did achieve later what it had planned then.

Yeddyurappa, who was the Opposition leader, was also a regular visitor to 'Anugraha' and the CM would be closeted with him for considerable lengths of time. I wondered why the CM didn't speak to Yeddyurappa himself and check the veracity of my information.

On December 2, the CM left for Delhi and I too reached Delhi the same evening. When I met him at Karnataka Bhavan, I told him that Deve Gowda is reported to be favouring expansion of the cabinet with only nine ministers. However, due to a variety of reasons, the expansion of the cabinet could not be finalised during that visit. On December 8, the CM met Deve Gowda at the residence of HD Revanna and once again discussed cabinet expansion and left for Delhi the same evening.

On the morning of December 9, I learnt that 37 MLAs of the JD(S) had met in a resort near Yelahanka and expressed their displeasure about not getting any important positions in the government. They were sore about the postponement of cabinet expansion and not appointing new chiefs for various government controlled boards and corporations.

Datta Peetha

As the days passed in December, I began worrying about the impending law and order problem in Chikmagalur district, because of the celebration of Datta Jayanti scheduled in that month and the attendant 'Datta Peetha' dispute. The celebration of this festival had earlier resulted in communal tensions necessitating heavy deployment of police force in the district. The problem was more or less akin to the Idgah Maidan dispute in Hubli which I have recounted earlier. Some people had termed the Datta Peetha issue as the 'Ayodhya of the South'.

Located close to Chikmagalur town is a hillock called Baba Budan Giri. Baba Budan, a Sufi saint, is said to have brought coffee to India from Saudi Arabia with him. He is said to have lived in a small cave in the hillock and performed several miracles. Hence the hill came to be named after him. His grave, along with two other Sufi saints, is situated in the cave. Hindus consider the same cave to be the abode of Lord Dattatreya, an incarnation of Brahma-Vishnu-Maheshwara and worship the holy sandals and the holy lamp of Dattatreya in the cave. The cave, which was being revered both by Hindus and Muslims, was never a point of dispute for more than a century. A descendant of the Baba, known as Shah Khadri or Sajjada used to manage the cave.

The Karnataka Government handed over the management of this shrine to the Wakf Board in the late 1960s. In 1978, a civil case was filed against the government over this matter and the dispute was agitated in various legal fora. Post-Ayodhya and post-Idgah Maidan disputes, the dispute about the ownership and management of the Baba Budan Giri shrine were raked up by Bajrang Dal, Vishwa Hindu Parishad, and many others. The issue reached a flashpoint in 1998 when some Hindu organisations declared that they would 'liberate' the Datta Peetha from the Muslims on December 3, 1998. 'Rath Yatras' were taken out from different parts of the State increasing communal tensions not only in the district but in other parts of the State. In later years, processions were organised to the shrine from all parts of Karnataka during the celebration of Datta Jayanti. The activists would also perform *havans* and other rituals near the cave. A month prior to the Jayanti, a ritual called Datta Mala Abhiyan would begin and devotees would be given a garland to wear indicating their intention to take part in the procession, which was termed as 'Shobha Yatra'.

During the 'Shobha Yatra' in December 2002, about 15,000 people participated which created anxiety in the minds of the local Muslim community. A large posse of policemen had to be deployed in the communally sensitive district weeks prior to the Jayanti. The prohibitory orders would be imposed and efforts would be made to prevent any attempt at destruction of the saint's *dargah* in the cave. Many persons, including me, thought that replays of 'Idgah Maidan' incidents were happening in Chikmagalur.

To oppose the Hindutva elements, an organisation called 'Komu Souharda Vedike' (Communal Harmony Forum) had come into existence and it had started mobilising people against the Hindu organisations. During the previous year when SM Krishna was the CM, journalist Gauri Lankesh, who was a member of the Vedike, along with Girish Karnad and other leaders had called on him and had demanded that the government should not give permission for that year's

'Shobha Yatra'. When the government granted permission to the organisers to go ahead with the Datta Jayanti celebrations and to hold the 'Shobha Yatra', the Vedike declared that it would bring together secular forces on the same day to hold a rally for communal harmony in Chikmagalur town. The police denied permission to the Vedike's programmes. On December 7 that year hundreds of Vedike activists had got arrested when they defied the prohibitory orders which were in force. These included journalist Gauri Lankesh, KL Ashok and other activists. They were lodged in jail.

With this in the background, Dharam Singh held several meetings with various persons and organisations to ensure peace during the forthcoming festival. Yeddyurappa along with a delegation of BJP legislators and others from Chikmagalur and Shimoga districts met the CM and requested him not to consider banning the 'Shobha Yatra' that year. The CM was non-committal.

Meanwhile, on December 12, the CM told me that three days later his cabinet would be expanded and that Congress high command had finalised the names of nine new ministers. I told him that it had taken a long time for this expansion and at least legislators would now be happy.

On December 15, some hours before the swearing-in ceremony, the JD(S) gave its list of 11 legislators. I was asked to contact each one of them and request them to attend the ceremony. With this induction of 20 ministers, the cabinet strength rose to 32, two short of the maximum 34 slots. I had guessed then that one of it would go to DK Shivakumar at the appropriate time.

In the meanwhile, the situation in Chikmagalur district was becoming tense with the Datta Jayanti approaching fast. Yeddyurappa and others had gone to Baba Budan Giri and later met the district administration demanding that too many restrictions should not be placed on the organisers. Pramod Mutalik, the rabble-rousing leader of Bajrang Dal and head of Sri Ram Sene, was taken into custody some days later.

After holding several rounds of meetings regarding maintenance of law and order in Chikmagalur district during Datta Jayanti festival the government decided to ban the 'Shobha Yatra'. On December 24, a State Transport bus was burnt in Sringeri in Chikmagalur district and the situation became very tense. Hundreds of VHP/Bajrang Dal activists were arrested. Chikmagalur bandh was called and the leader in the vanguard of Datta Jayanti celebrations CT Ravi was also arrested.

Datta Jayanti, however, passed off without any serious problem that year and we all heaved a sigh of relief.

Many people didn't know that Dharam Singh, like Atal Bihari Vajpayee, was born on December 25. Though a big birthday bash had been planned for the day, the CM was not in a celebratory mood as he had to attend the funeral of former Prime Minister PV Narasimha Rao at Hyderabad later in the day. Dharam Singh who had studied in Hyderabad was reverential towards Rao. When I was the SP of Gulbarga district in 1985, Rao, then the Union HRD Minister, had visited Gulbarga and had told me about his connections to the district.

The CM led a delegation from Bangalore for the funeral. He invited Deve Gowda to join him, but I was told that Gowda refused to join as the delegation was using a private aircraft belonging to liquor baron Vijay Mallya for their trip to Hyderabad.

The very next day Tsunami hit the coast of Tamil Nadu and we all got busy with sending relief materials to the affected persons.

Firefight

As the year 2004 came to an end, I thought that the coalition government was mostly indulging in firefighting resulting in work related to the development of the State taking a beating. Problems after problems surfaced which had to be tackled with utmost patience and tact. I believed that only a person with the mental make-up of Dharam Singh could brave the storm and run the government. He had a way with people. He didn't antagonise anyone. He would often tell me that a leader should concentrate more on enemies than his friends. He always tried to keep the opposition party leaders in good humour. Probably that was the reason that he would meet the then Leader of Opposition Yeddyurappa very frequently and attend to most of his requests in a positive manner.

People, however, perceived Dharam Singh differently. They thought that the CM was yielding too much to the pressures and pulls of Deve Gowda and believed that it was Deve Gowda who was running the government and not Dharam Singh. Being indebted to Deve Gowda for his position, Dharam Singh had to oblige many of the requests coming from Gowda and his family members. But many times he stood his ground firmly. I am aware that he had earlier brushed aside suggestions to get me replaced. A mention must be made about posting a particular 'heavy weight' officer of a prominent community as IGP of Central Range, Bangalore. The JD(S) leaders, on coming to know about the impending posting, mounted tremendous pressure on the CM not to post the said officer as the IG of the range, a stronghold of the JD(S). But Dharam Singh did not budge and the officer was posted to the same range.

The most contentious issue between the coalition partners those days related to transfer of government officials. The ministers from JD(S) would not entertain requests of transfers of officials working in their departments from the Congress leaders and the Congress Ministers would do likewise with the requests from JD(S) leaders. Many of the requests from Deve Gowda and his family made to the CM were related to posting and transfers of officers.

At this juncture, I must mention that the CM had made me a points man with respect to the subject of police transfers. Whenever any legislator came to him with a request for transfer of any police officer from the level of Sub-Inspector to the level of Deputy Superintendent of Police, the CM would immediately convey the request to me if I was around. The CM would tell the concerned legislator in my presence that I would get things done and would hand over the request note to me. If I were away, he would talk to one of his assistants around him to communicate the request to me. It was my duty to talk to the DG and IGP or the concerned Additional DGP Administration and get the orders issued. I was also supposed to inform the CM of the compliance of his orders.

On receipt such requests, I would consult Achuta Rao, the Additional DGP in-charge of Administration in the office of the DG and IGP. Both of us would get the service records of the concerned officer and ascertain whether the request could be acceded to. Later on, both of us would meet the CM and convey the viewpoint of the police department and seek his final orders. Only in rare cases, the CM would insist on posting the officer concerned to the places where the legislators wanted. As regards transfer of IPS officers, I would first consult SV Ranganath and later on with the Home Secretary and the DG and IGP. Later on, both Ranganath and I would brief the CM and get his specific orders on the transfer.

Frequent transfers of police officers, more so at the request of legislators and political bigwigs, had brought a bad name to the CM. When I mentioned this to the CM, he expressed his helplessness in stating that he was bound to listen to the requests of elected representatives and cannot brush them aside. At that time I reminded him that during the tenure of Gundu Rao as the CM, there was absolutely no political interference in police transfers. The CM mentioned that he was running a coalition government and cannot take a very rigid stand. Unfortunately those days, the Supreme Court had not yet given its orders on the subject of police transfers. It was years later that Karnataka Police Act was amended by which it became impossible to transfer a police officer prematurely.

It was not the nature of Singh to nurse a grievance against anybody. As mentioned earlier, he went out of his way to please his enemies. To cite an example, in his home constituency of Jewargi, Singh's closest rival used to be Shivalingappa Patil Naribol. Naribol had contested against Singh thrice, twice from the BJP, in 1994, 1999 and 2004 and had lost. In 2004, he had narrowly missed defeating Singh. When Naribol died on January 23, 2005, Singh made it a point to go to Gulbarga and pay his last respects. Because of such a nature, Singh used to be called as *Ajatashatru*, a person with no enemies.

It is interesting to note that Shivalingappa's son Doddappa Gowda Patil Naribol of the BJP defeated Singh by 52 votes in the 2008 assembly polls. For the first time since 1978, Singh had lost any Legislative Assembly elections. The entire Jewargi constituency was shocked and numb with disbelief then.

After Dharam Singh became the CM, nature too became kinder towards Karnataka. There were copious rains after years of drought and with this many problems got sorted out automatically. We looked forward to a peaceful and prosperous time ahead. But it was not to be.

10

Naxal Problem Takes Centre-Stage

The year 2005 began with the CM, Dharam Singh getting annoyed with me without any valid reason. On the evening of January 1, the CM was supposed to go to an ashram in Bidadi along with SM Krishna. Due to a miscommunication on the part of his OSD, Krishna, having waited for the CM to come to his house, had left for the ashram and the CM missed the programme. This had upset the CM and I was unaware of this.

Around 5 PM, I had called the CM's media officer HB Dinesh for some information. As we were speaking, the CM who was said to be standing next to Dinesh took the phone from him and told me about missing his visit to the ashram. Not knowing the background, I replied that he had done a good thing as the ashram was supposed to be involved in a land dispute. On hearing this, he suddenly flared up, shouted at me and disconnected the call.

At about 9 PM, the CM called me and enquired about the despatch of relief materials to Tsunami victims in the Andamans. When I expressed my lack of knowledge about it, he once again became furious and summoned me to his house. He had cooled down by the time I met him. I got in touch with the officer who was in-charge of the relief operations and gave the CM the relevant information and returned home late in the night.

The next morning, when I met Dharam Singh, he told me that SM Krishna, being a very sensitive person, would have mistaken the CM for not joining him for the ashram visit. He told me that SM Krishna was a senior leader of the party and that he had served under him as a minister until very recently and that his action would be perceived as impertinence. I told the CM that I would meet SM Krishna and clarify that whatever was done by the CM was unintentional.

Later I spoke to Sridhar, OSD to Krishna, and told him that I would like to meet Krishna, and clarify the previous evening's incident. He told me that Dharam Singh had already spoken to him and clarified and thus the matter was closed.

As I disconnected the phone, I remembered that I had annoyed Krishna too a few months ago when he was proceeding to the Bidadi ashram with his wife. A smile crossed my lips.

Evangelist Benny Hinn

During the next two weeks, the subject that took centre-stage was the Benny Hinn programme slated to be held in Bangalore. Israeli-American evangelist, Toufik Benedictus 'Benny' Hinn used to organise in huge stadia all around the world, what he called 'faith healing summits'. He claimed that he had the power given by God to transmit miracles by which he would cure people of various physical ailments. He would gather huge crowds and his television programmes had been super-hits. He had desired to organise one such meeting in Bangalore. The organisers had sought the government permission to hold the meeting at the Jakkur airfield.

After several meetings to discuss the various ramifications about the programme like maintenance of law and order, traffic management, providing security to Benny Hinn and the organisers, it was decided to give permission to hold the programme.

Immediately thereafter, a huge controversy arose over the permission given to the organisers by the government. Many groups felt that in the name of faith healing, conversions to Christianity would take place. Some individuals took objection to the publication of pamphlets in connection with the programme which had purportedly castigated idol worship. A number of complaints were filed against the organisers and Public Interest Litigations were filed in the Karnataka High Court.

The BJP took strong objection for giving permission to organise the programme. State-wide protests were held. Some leaders of the BJP compared Hinn to Aslam 'Blade' Baba of Bijapur who had cheated a number of gullible people claiming to cure them of their chronic illnesses and had been arrested by police. Some BJP leaders also sat on a *dharna* in front of the statue of Mahatma Gandhi in Cubbon Park.

The CM who had been to Delhi on January 19, 2005 for a discussion with the Planning Commission, seemed to have sounded his party bosses about the show. He returned to Bangalore late in the night. The next day the Legislature Session began and the BJP members walked out in protest against Benny Hinn show.

I had received inputs that there would be serious law and order problems in Bangalore on January 21 and had alerted the Police Commissioner to take necessary precautionary measures. Bakrid festival was slated to be held the next day and police had to organise bandobust for the same. Meanwhile, a call for Bangalore bundh had been given to protest against the Benny Hinn show. To top it, the President of Chile was visiting the city and the police were really hard pressed to maintain order. I expected violence to break out on January 21 and kept my fingers crossed.

The show went off peacefully. The Bangalore Police had successfully managed public order. Those persons who attended the show described it as 'mere show and nothing else'. They stated that several persons who had come to the event hoping to get a cure for their diseases had gone back disappointed.

On January 22, the CM left for Gulbarga in the morning. As he was returning the same evening, I had gone to the airport to receive him. While waiting for the CM's helicopter, I saw another helicopter on the tarmac and when I went near it, I saw my colleague IPS officer Gopal Hosur there. He greeted me and told me that the helicopter was being used by Benny Hinn to go to Jakkur airfield. Meanwhile, Hinn came there. He was wearing a very flashy dress. Hosur introduced him to me and Hinn shook hands with me and invited me to his programme. I excused myself by mumbling that I had some important work to attend.

Many people had claimed that a mere touch of Benny Hinn would be an invigorating experience. I didn't experience that. Meanwhile, the CM returned from Gulbarga and later on, he went to Jakkur and attended the show. Fortunately, nothing untoward happened the second day also and the entire event was soon forgotten.

Naxal Encounter

On February 6, I learnt that an encounter between Naxals and police had taken place in Menasinahadya in Chikmagalur district in which two Naxals had been killed and some policemen injured. On speaking to BK Singh, the SP of the district, I learnt that the persons killed were Saket Rajan, the topmost Naxalite leader of the State, and Shivalingu hailing from Raichur district. I immediately spoke to the CM about this incident and explained to him how the death of Saket Rajan would be a big blow for the Naxal movement in Karnataka.

The next day, a delegation came to meet the CM to protest against what they called as a fake police encounter in Menasinahadya. The delegation, called as Citizens' Initiative for Peace, was led by Gauri Lankesh. It comprised of Prof G Ramakrishna, and advocate Ravi Varma Kumar. The delegation demanded a judicial enquiry into the encounter and also wanted that a second post-mortem conducted on the bodies of the two deceased in Bangalore. The CM agreed for the second post-mortem examination but stated that he would order a magisterial enquiry by senior IAS officer Chiranjiv Singh and not a judicial enquiry.

I must digress here. As the chief of Intelligence, I was aware that journalist Gauri Lankesh was involved in a number of social causes including those related to Naxals, who were at that time quite active in the Western Ghats. We had also known that she had attended one of the press briefings organised deep inside the Western Ghats by Saket Rajan in 2004 along with other journalists. She was known to have left-leaning views and a mention has already been made about her association with Komu Souharda Vedike which had agitated against 'Shobha Yatra' and other issues connected with Datta Peetha in Chikmagalur district.

As the CM was going to Mangalore the same afternoon, I decided to go with him and see the scene of the encounter to get more details. After reaching Mangalore, I visited the hospital where the injured police constable AM Satish had been admitted. Two bullets had been recovered from his thigh. He appeared to be cheerful and explained to me how the encounter took place. He stated that on getting information that some Naxals were visiting a house in Menasinahadya, a team of police officials led by Deputy Superintendent of Police Shivakumar and Inspector Srinidhi had laid in wait for them. A few hours before dawn, they saw a group of armed persons walking on a hillock in front of them and when challenged, they opened fire on the police party resulting in the encounter. After wishing him a speedy recovery, I went to Kudremukh and halted for the night.

The next morning I visited the scene of the encounter and had a detailed discussion with the SP about how the encounter took place. The bodies of the two deceased had been sent to Bangalore for a second post-mortem at Bowring Hospital. After gathering all the information, I returned to Mangalore and accompanied the CM on his journey to Bangalore. On our return to Bangalore, we visited the hospital to which the injured Inspector had been shifted. The CM learnt about the details of the encounter from the Inspector Srinidhi.

Later on, the CM held a meeting of senior officers regarding security arrangements to be made for the impending visit of the Prime Minister Dr Manmohan Singh to Karnataka. Later on, Gauri Lankesh met the CM and demanded that the bodies of the two slain Naxals be handed over to them for the last rites. The CM agreed for this request and asked the Addl DGP in-charge of Law and Order Subhash Bharani to do the needful. Both Bharani and the DG and IGP Borkar were opposed to the idea and were very firm that they would not hand over the bodies to anyone other than the close relatives of the deceased. A senior police officer in Mysore met Saket Rajan's mother in Mysore but she was not interested in performing the last rites of her son who had left home decades ago. I was told that she had given a letter to this effect. The other deceased Naxal's parents who were from a remote village in North Karnataka had left for Bangalore. Both the bodies were cremated in Bangalore by some officials under police supervision and the ashes were handed over to the parents of Shivalingu and representatives of Citizens' Initiative for Peace (CIP). This action by the police was lawful.

The very next day the representatives of Citizens' Initiative for Peace wanted to come in a procession with the urn containing the ashes of the deceased Naxals and meet the CM. The Bangalore Police Commissioner refused them permission to take out a procession. The delegation later met the CM at his home office where I was also present. The delegation had the 'Revolutionary Balladeer' from Andhra, Gaddar, and Andhra poet Vara Vara Rao, apart from Gauri Lankesh and others. They demanded the suspension of DG and IGP Borkar for not handing over the bodies of the deceased to the CIP. The CM listened to them patiently but did not promise them anything.

Policemen Killed by Naxals

At the stroke of midnight on February 10, I was woken up by the operator of the Police Control Room to inform me that a group of Naxals had attacked a police post at Venkatammanahalli in Tumkur district killing several policemen and escaping with their weapons. Six policemen including an officer of Karnataka State Reserve Police and a civilian had been shot dead. The police officials were sleeping in their makeshift camp which was a school building located at the outskirts of the village. After Naxals had exchanged fire with the police at Venkatammanahalli village in April 2003, a platoon of the Karnataka State Reserve Police had been deployed there.

Even during the long drawn Veerappan operations, not so many police personnel from Karnataka had been martyred in one single incident and for the Karnataka Police, it was definitely a black day.

Located in Pavagada taluk which had seen a lot of Naxal activity for nearly three decades, Venkatammanahalli bordered Anantapur district of Andhra Pradesh. Some years ago the vehicle of an excise contractor had been attacked and arms and ammunition being carried by its escort party had been looted by Naxals at Tirumani in the same taluk. A former Naxal leader and Telugu Desam MLA for Penukonda in Andhra Pradesh, Paritala Ravindra, had contributed to the rise of Naxalism in that taluk for three decades. Ravindra had been a minister in Andhra Pradesh and had been shot dead on January 24 the same year.

The very first doubt that crossed my mind was whether this attack was an act of revenge for the killing of Saket Rajan in the police encounter. Many others also had similar apprehension. I was very much worried about the ramifications of this incident as the Prime Minister was arriving in Bangalore that very day and was going to Mysore to attend two different programmes.

On the morning of February 11, I met the CM and told him that most of my colleagues in the police department were extremely shocked about this attack and were blaming him for displaying a soft policy towards the Naxals. I briefed him that the killing of so many policemen was reminiscent of attacks by forest brigand Veerappan and most personnel of Karnataka Reserve Police were angry with the government. I mentioned that his decision to agree to handover the body of Saket Rajan to the representatives of Citizens' Initiative for Peace had not gone well with the police top brass. The police had not implemented this decision, though.

Reminding him that his decision to grant a piece of government land in Chikmagalur district to erect a 'Martyr's Column' to commemorate the Naxals who had died in police action had been criticised by Yeddyurappa, I told him that Deve Gowda had warned that if Naxalism is not nipped in the bud, it would engulf the entire State. I told him that if he didn't act tough, he may have to face the wrath of the entire police force and no government could afford to take that risk.

The CM was visibly shocked after listening to me. He decided to immediately call a high-level meeting of senior officials to review the security of the State. At the meeting which was held a few hours later, he announced that the government would tackle the Naxal problem effectively and that he would talk to the Naxals only if they laid down arms. He also agreed to establish a special force to handle this problem.

Meanwhile, the chiefs of Intelligence of Andhra Pradesh and Tamil Nadu phoned me and sought details of the Venkatammanahalli incident. As the place of the incident was very close to Andhra Pradesh, I sought the help of Arvinda Rao, ADG Intelligence, Andhra Pradesh, in solving the case and nabbing the culprits apart from the recovery of the stolen police weapons. He asked me to visit Hyderabad for further discussions.

The same afternoon the bodies of the martyrs were brought to the office of the DG and IGP. The CM paid homage to the martyrs. His delay in reaching the office of the DG and IGP by more than an hour, due to a pressing prior engagement, was not liked by many police officers and men who had gathered in the premises of the DG and IGP's office.

That evening the family members of Karnataka State Reserve Police personnel went on a rampage near their housing colony in Koramangala, Bangalore protesting against the "failure of the government in not giving adequate protection to the KSRP camp." They set fire to petty shops and buses in their vicinity which necessitated the deployment of the Central Reserve Police Force to bring the situation under control. As far as I knew, except in the year 1980, Karnataka Police had never shown their dissent in public and hence I was terribly worried over this turn of events. As I too had worked as the Additional DGP of KSRP only a few years ago, I was alarmed.

KSRP men, I was aware, were upset about the 'meagre' rewards given by the State Government for those involved in Veerappan operations. They had formed the bulk of Karnataka Special Task Force set up to nab Veerappan and their grievance was that they were not given rewards like their counterparts in Tamil Nadu.

As the police were trying to control the situation at Koramangala, the PM arrived in Bangalore along with his wife and reached Raj Bhavan where he was staying for the night.

The next morning, I joined the PM's entourage on his visit to Suttur and Mysore. Addressing the media at Bangalore, the PM, who was aware of the Venkatammanahalli incident, said that though Naxalism had to be tackled by the State Government, the Centre would give the State a helping hand.

After the departure of the PM, the CM held a series of review meetings regarding curbing Naxalism in general and the incident at Venkatammanahalli in particular. The next day, I went to Hyderabad, met the CM Dr YS Rajasekhara Reddy and sought the co-operation of his government in tackling the Naxal menace in Karnataka. It was public knowledge that Andhra Pradesh, which had been severely affected by Naxalism for decades had effectively controlled the problem and was considered a 'model' by States affected by Left Wing Extremism.

I mentioned to Dr Reddy, that when he was studying Medicine in Gulbarga, I had started my career as an IPS officer there. I also told him that while he as Andhra CM had studied in our State, our CM, Dharam Singh had studied in Hyderabad. Dr Reddy smiled. He spoke to me in Kannada and assured full co-operation from his government in solving the Venkatammanahalli case. He told me, "You have come here because we have created the problem."

I returned to Bangalore and met the CM and briefed him about my visit. The CM told me that he had decided to visit Venkatammanahalli. My first reaction was surprise because Pavagada taluk was considered a jinxed place by most politicians. The talk was that any Chief Minister who visited that taluk would lose his seat. I didn't mention this to the CM but told him that we need to beef up security there if he were to visit the taluk. I also told him that it is better if he went there by helicopter as the road journey would be very unsafe. He asked me to tell the DG and IGP to make suitable security arrangements.

Land Mines

Meanwhile, we learnt that a number of land mines had been planted on various roads leading to Venkatammanahalli and that police had recovered a few under a culvert. By looking at the mines, it was obvious that they had been kept there months ago. This was the classic *modus operandi* of Naxals from Andhra. They would normally choose some culverts on important arterial roads and place mines under them and keep quiet for a long time. Whenever they came to know about a VIP travelling by that road, they would activate the mines and blast the VIP convoy when it crossed the culvert through remote control devices.

I was told by our officers that even if the CM performed his journey by helicopter he still would have to travel by road for some distance. The incident of blasting through land mines the convoy of the then Andhra CM Chandrababu Naidu by Naxals at the foothills of Tirupathi immediately came to my mind. The CM was, therefore, advised to cancel his proposed visit to Venkatammanahalli. With great reluctance, he agreed.

When I went to the village sometime later, I was shocked to notice how our men had become sitting ducks to the Naxal group which had arrived at the camp a little before midnight in five vehicles - three mini-lorries, a van, and a jeep and had shot dead the sentry at the gate and fired at another sentry on the roof of the building. They threw bombs inside the two classrooms where the KSRP personnel were sleeping. The attack had taken everyone by surprise and the policemen didn't have adequate time to react. It was quite obvious that the attack was meticulously planned.

In May 2005, Naxals struck again. On the night of May 17, about 15 Naxals went to the residence of Sheshappa, a farmer in Menasinahadya of Chikmagalur district and brutally killed him suspecting him to be a police informer. The manner of his killing shocked everyone. Menasinahadya was the same village where Saket Rajan and Shivalingu had been killed in an encounter a few months ago. The police suspected that the killing of Sheshappa was a revenge killing, probably due to the suspicion that he had informed the police regarding the presence of Saket Rajan in that village.

The Naxals struck again in Udupi district two months later. On July 28, two jeeps and van carrying police personnel were on their way from Kokkanabettu to Mutlupady in the district when the landmines were detonated around 4.30 PM. The first mine detonated after the first jeep passed, the second after the second jeep passed and the third after the van passed. Thirteen policemen were travelling in the two jeeps and there were 15 personnel of the Karnataka State Reserve Police (KSRP) in the van. The blasts damaged the jeeps and eight police personnel in them were injured, two of them with head injuries.

After the detonation of the landmines, there was an exchange of fire between the police party and the Naxals. The Naxals opened fire first and the police returned fire. There were about 12-15 Naxals who were firing from a distance, and the exchange of fire went on for quite some time. What surprised me was that we in the Intelligence Wing had definite information about such an attack and we had sent written warning to the district police. Obviously, our warnings had not been taken seriously. It was pure luck that no policeman had been killed as it happened in Venkatammanahalli.

On receiving this news, I went to the Legislative Assembly where the CM was attending the session and informed him. He asked me to brief the opposition leaders about the incident and hence a meeting was called in the chambers of the Speaker where I gave details of the incident to the leaders.

Many legislators expressed apprehension about their own safety and the very next day raised this issue in the House and demanded protection to the Legislators from the Malnad area.

Fortunately after July 2005, till I remained as Addl DG Intelligence, no serious incident involving the Naxals took place in the State.

11

Congress Faces Electoral Defeats

By April 2005, the political situation had become quite precarious. It was obvious to any onlooker that the relationship between the coalition partners was not cordial, to say the least. The organisation of a rally called 'Daridranarayana Rally' by the JD(S) targeting slum dwellers, daily wage workers, and other oppressed classes did not go well with the Congress. The Karnataka Pradesh Congress Committee President, Janardhana Poojary, raised serious objections for this rally and called for its cancellation. But the brain behind the rally, HD Deve Gowda, was adamant and went ahead.

On April 30, veteran journalist Shekhar Gupta wrote in the *Indian Express* that Dharam Singh was a weak CM and the coalition government would fall by the year-end. When I drew the CM's attention to this observation, I was surprised to note that he agreed with the assessment about the imminent fall of the government. Within a week bye-elections to the State Legislative Assembly from the Chamarajpet constituency in Bangalore and to the Lok Sabha from Shimoga constituency were announced. I thought that both the coalition partners would concentrate on fighting elections and not fight each other.

As expected, the Congress nominated its former MLA RV Devraj to contest from Chamarajpet. JD(S) nominated a transport operator Zameer Ahmed Khan. The BJP made it a triangular fight by nominating Pramila Nesargi. Similarly, in

Shimoga, it was Ayanur Manjunath from the Congress, LT Timmappa Hegde from the JD(S) and Bhanu Prakash from the BJP. An interesting feature in Shimoga was that the former CM of Karnataka S Bangarappa was contesting as a candidate from the Samajwadi Party. Ayanur Manjunath was the choice of Dharam Singh.

In the second week of May, there was a flurry of activity among the IPS officers. The DG and IGP Borkar was retiring by the month-end and his successor had to be chosen. This would also involve top-level changes among the IPS officers and lobbying for plum posts began. Many senior officers began meeting the CM with their requests.

For the post of DG and IGP, three officers were under consideration. In terms of seniority, they were, BNP Albuquerque (1969 batch of IPS), BS Sial (1971) and KR Srinivasan (1972). As the City Police Commissioner Mariswamy was also getting elevated to the post of DGP, the Commissioner's post also had also to be filled up. Except for one officer, none approached the CM to lobby for that post as far as I knew.

New DG and IGP

The CM had already indicated to me in private that he would be posting Albuquerque as the next DG and IGP. He said that apart from being the seniormost officer, he also belonged to a minority community. The CM said, "if he is not appointed as DG and IGP, my detractors would go to Madam Sonia Gandhi and complain that while I posted MD Singh, who is perceived to be of my caste, as the DGP, I overlooked a Christian. Besides, he would be retiring soon."

On May 31, Sonia Gandhi was visiting Karwar and the CM was there to receive her. After the function in Karwar, he was scheduled to go to Sagar in Shimoga district for overseeing the election arrangements and return to Bangalore by evening. As Borkar had to handover charge as DG and IGP that afternoon, the orders appointing the new DG and IGP had to be issued at least by 3 PM. Hence SV Ranganath, Secretary to the CM, telephoned him about the issuance of orders. The CM told him that he would return to Bangalore and pass his orders on file. Around 2 PM, Ranganath contacted him again and told him that as the matter was urgent, the CM could tell the name of the person chosen by him over the phone, and after the issuance of orders could sign the concerned file. The CM didn't agree and insisted on return to Bangalore and sign the file.

When at 3 PM, the CM was still in Sagar, Ranganath and I spoke to him and asked him that he could write the name of the new DGP on a paper and send it through fax. He didn't agree and said that he was starting from Sagar and would arrive in Bangalore by 5 PM, before the office hours. He took off from Sagar in his helicopter by 3.15 PM. We reckoned that his copter would land around 4.15 PM and both of us went to receive him at HAL airport. Ranganath had carried the file regarding DG and IGP's appointment in his hand.

Around 3.45 PM, the CM's OSD Krishnaiah called me on my cell phone and said that he was with the CM in the helicopter and due to bad weather the helicopter may land in Tumkur. He wanted me to alert the SP of Tumkur district and make arrangements for a vehicle to bring them to Bangalore. He also told me that the battery of his cell phone was getting weak and he may not be able to make or receive any call. I alerted the police control room for the needful to be done.

By then it started raining very heavily in Bangalore and we learnt that Tumkur also had copious rains. Both Ranganath and I went to 'Anugraha' and were waiting for the call from Tumkur. Meanwhile as was the practice top police officers had gathered in the office of the DG and IGP to receive the new Head of the Police Force. Every officer was in his ceremonial uniform. The entire police force was curious to know the name of their new leader and I was bombarded with calls from my colleagues as to when the order for the new HoPF (Head of Police Force) would be issued. However, none of the officers in the reckoning called me.

At about 4.15 PM the SP of Tumkur spoke to me and told me that the CM's helicopter didn't land in Tumkur and he had learnt that it had flown towards Bangalore. He informed me that the weather was too foul for any helicopter to land in Tumkur. In Bangalore also there were heavy rains. I was terribly worried about the CM's safety. I started getting morbid thoughts. I was in constant touch with the Bangalore airport to know about the helicopter location.

At about 5.30 PM, we got a call from Krishnaiah that the helicopter had landed safely in the Air Force Station near Mehkri circle and asked the vehicles to be sent there. Ranganath and I heaved a sigh of relief. A fully drenched Dharam Singh arrived at his residence at 6 PM.

The first thing he did on arrival was to ask for the file of DG and IGP's appointment. He wrote the name of Albuquerque on the file with his left hand. (Many do not know that Singh was a southpaw-left handed.) Ranganath immediately spoke to the Secretary of the Personnel Department (who had been specifically requested to remain in office beyond office hours only to issue the appointment orders of the new DGP). Later on Ranganath and I contacted Albuquerque, broke the news, congratulated him and requested him to assume charge of the post of DG and IGP immediately.

When the CM went to his room to change, I asked Krishnaiah as to why they did not land in Tumkur. He stated that the CM was very keen to sign the DGP's orders and asked the helicopter pilot to proceed to Bangalore. During the journey, the rains and wind had severely lashed the CM's helicopter and only due to the dexterity of the pilot they could land safely at the first visible helipad in the Air Force Station.

Till date, neither Ranganath nor I know the reason behind the CM's insistence on signing the relevant file in Bangalore. Strange are the ways of people who govern.

What Krishnaiah recounted later needs to be taken with a pinch of salt. He mentioned that when the CM's helicopter landed at the Air Force Station, the security personnel of the

Air Force thought it to be an intruder helicopter and surrounded it with pointed weapons. Only when they saw the CM slowly getting down, they relaxed and offered the CM a cup of tea.

Albuquerque came to 'Anugraha' in his ceremonial uniform at 7.30 PM and thanked the CM. He took charge as the DG and IGP around 8 PM.

Shock for Congress

The bye-elections took place on June 2. When the results were announced the Congress was in for a shock. Bangarappa had defeated the Congress candidate by a margin of 16,000 votes for the Shimoga Lok Sabha seat. In the Chamarajpet Assembly constituency, Zameer Ahmed Khan of the JD(S) defeated RV Devraj by 3,500 votes. It was definitely a political setback for the CM. While in my report I had stated that Bangarappa had an edge in Shimoga, the CM had felt that the Congress candidate might win by a small margin. The defeat of Devaraj in Chamarajpet was not predicted by the State Intelligence. It came as a surprise to me.

The electoral defeat in both the places made Dharam Singh sulk. He was very hopeful of Ayanur Manjunath winning in Shimoga and kept telling me that his own partymen had ditched him. The election results also seemed to change the equation between the coalition partners. Rumours started circulating that the CM may be replaced.

Meanwhile, pressure started mounting on the CM to effect the promotion and transfer of IPS officers. When the CM told me that Kumaraswamy had requested him to replace me from the post of Intelligence Chief and had also demanded that Bharani should not be posted as Commissioner of Police, Bangalore, I asked the CM whether Kumaraswamy had given him any reason for my shift. The CM didn't offer me the reason. I guessed that Kumaraswamy and several JD(S) leaders might be unhappy with me in not getting the postings of various officers as demanded by them by insisting on it with the CM.

On the morning of June 7, when I went to brief the CM at 'Anugraha', I saw Siddaiah, Secretary to CM, sitting with Singh. The CM was looking at a file. I was told that the file pertained to the posting of Bangalore Police Commissioner. Siddaiah told the CM to post me as the next Commissioner and the CM looked at me. I told them that the incumbent Mariswamy, who was being promoted and posted out, belonged to 1972 batch of IPS, whereas I belonged to the 1976 batch. If I were to be appointed as the Commissioner, I would be superseding six officers in the IPS and this would not go well with my colleagues. Siddaiah shot back saying that the post of the Commissioner is of ADGP rank and as I was holding that rank, there was nothing wrong in appointing me to that post. I told both of them that if I were to be appointed to the coveted post, I would have to face sniggers and innuendos as many officers would attribute my getting the post because of being close to CM as the Chief of Intelligence. I told both of them that I would rather wait for my turn and avoid being called a *chamcha*. Both of them were surprised. Dr Ajai Kumar Singh of the 1974 batch was posted as Commissioner of Police, Bangalore and Mariswamy was promoted as DGP Home Guards and Fire Force.

About eight months earlier too a similar situation had arisen. A proposal was before the Chief Minister Krishna to transfer Mariswamy and the CM was mulling over the matter. At that time, Principal Secretary Jairaj told me that he had suggested my name for the Commissioner's post. I had given Jairaj, the same reason which I gave to Siddaiah. As the matter regarding the transfer of the Bangalore Police Commissioner was dropped by Krishna then, Mariswamy had continued in his post.

Siddaramaiah Shown the Door

A few days later, strong rumours started circulating that Siddaramaiah, Deputy CM, would be shown the door by the JD(S). There were also rumours that he would be joining the

Congress party. It came as a surprise to me as my colleagues had not been able to gather this piece of Intelligence. Kumaraswamy spoke to me and told me that if Siddaramaiah was to be admitted to the Congress, the coalition government would break up the same day. Many Congressmen, who spoke to me later, told me that Siddaramaiah would be an asset to the Congress party and deserved to be admitted to the party. When I told them that it would probably break the coalition government, they welcomed such an event. As if to give credence to rumours Siddaramaiah reportedly met Sonia Gandhi in the last week of June.

Gowda wanted the CM to completely sideline Siddaramaiah and to consult him on all important transfers of government officials. The JD(S) leaders wanted that they should also be consulted in policy decisions related to the departments which were run by Ministers from the Congress too. The Congress legislators too were unhappy that they were being ignored by the JD(S) ministers.

On June 30, Dr HC Mahadevappa, a close confidant of Siddaramaiah, met me and informed me that Deve Gowda had spoken to Yeddyurappa and was trying to forge an alliance with the BJP. He also stated that the JD(S) was headed for a split. Siddaramaiah along with a dozen legislators would bid goodbye to the JD(S), he said. I passed on this crucial information to the CM the same day.

Despite the understanding reached between Sonia Gandhi and Gowda, many Congressmen in the State were quite unhappy with the alliance and wanted it to break. Many members of Parliament and legislators whom I used to meet routinely were of the opinion that it is better to have the President's Rule than face humiliation in the hands of JD(S). I had learnt that some of the Congress leaders were trying to get the BJP legislators split and form a new coalition government.

July 2005 was a period in which the CM was constantly under tension. Many of his party members started showing defiance towards him openly. Some demanded a change of leadership alleging that Singh had become a puppet of Deve Gowda. Some of them were openly and deliberately making statements against Deve Gowda and his sons and sometimes against the JD(S) with the intention that such action might finally lead to a breaking of the alliance.

On July 13, when the appointment of Mallikarjuna Kharge as the new President of the KPCC was announced, the CM was most surprised because he had not been taken into confidence by the high command before the announcement. The CM had an excellent relationship with the earlier President Janardhan Poojary and Poojary's unexpected change came as a blow to the CM.

Dharam Singh never expected that Poojary would be replaced so early. He also least expected Kharge to head the KPCC because it was the earlier practice in the party not to have two leaders from the same district to head important positions - the Party Chief and the CM. The appointment was perceived as a message by the Party to the JD(S) that it cannot have any say in the internal affairs of the Congress party. Moreover, Kharge was a very strong leader having a large following and would have his say in important matters. He was also an aspirant to the post of CM, along with Singh when the coalition government was formed. The other prominent aspirants, apart from Krishna, were RV Deshpande, HK Patil, and Oscar Fernandes.

On hearing about Kharge's appointment, the CM expected that it may be a signal for his replacement. He surmised that either Margaret Alva or Oscar Fernandes might replace him and hence became worried.

CM Rebuffed by the Party

The fact that he was not informed by the party leaders about Rahul Gandhi's visit to Bangalore on July 14, though private, had also embarrassed Dharam Singh. Rahul Gandhi visited the ISKCON temple in Bangalore, met Sudha Murthy and left for Hubli later. We were told that RV Deshpande went to Hubli after casting his vote in the elections to the Legislative Council held that day to be with Rahul Gandhi who was also visiting Haliyal, the constituency of Deshpande.

Even for the selection of the party candidate for the Council election, which was necessitated by the resignation of RV Devraj, the CM had been rebuffed by his party high command. Devraj had earlier facilitated the election of SM Krishna, his mentor, to contest from the Chamarajpet assembly constituency in 2004. As compensation, he had been accommodated in the Legislative Council later. Again when Krishna vacated his assembly seat to become the Governor of Maharashtra, Devraj was chosen as the party candidate for the Chamarajpet Assembly seat which he lost to the JD(S) candidate.

When the bye-election to the Legislative Council was announced, the CM had desired that KK Murthy be considered for the seat. Murthy was not only his close friend but had the support of Deve Gowda. When the party high command didn't agree to the CM's suggestion and fielded RV Venkatesh, the CM was thoroughly disappointed. To rub the salt on the wound, some detractors of the CM had told Murthy that the CM did not canvass hard to convince the party high command to make Murthy the party candidate. Though KK Murthy was quite disappointed, he continued to be the trusted emissary between Deve Gowda and the CM.

The elections were held on July 15. As the JD(S) didn't field any candidate, Venkatesh won quite easily.

The continued inaction by the party high command in not reining in the partymen who were openly supporting the AHINDA (Kannada acronym for **A**lpasankhyataru - minorities, **HIN**dulidavaru - backward classes, and **DA**litaru - Scheduled Castes) movement of Siddaramaiah had worried the CM as much as it worried Deve Gowda. Though the party high command had given an assurance that a statement asking the party workers not to attend AHINDA rally would be issued, the top Congress leaders didn't make any such statement which indicated that the CM was not getting what he wanted.

Transfer 'Business'

Because of the political situation, governance had almost come to a standstill during that period. Most of the bureaucrats were of the opinion that the only work being done by the government was postings and transfers of officials. Normally transfers of officials happen only once a year, usually before the beginning of the academic year for schools and colleges. But those days, transfers were taking place at the whims and fancies of the legislators especially in the departments of Public Works, Police, Revenue and Municipal Administration. Because two different parties were governing, every transfer of key officials in the taluk and district level would pose a problem. Many a time an officer transferred to a particular post would be transferred out within a period of six months thanks to a rival who was angling for the same post. It was like a game of musical chairs. Since the officials were unable to settle down with work, no files moved.

The Police Department, according to me, was the worst affected. Every MLA wanted to have his crony to be the SHO in the police stations functioning in his constituency. He would, therefore, give 'minutes' (a brief note) to the Home Minister, who used to be the CM himself and get the officer of his choice posted. To get 'lucrative' postings for themselves unscrupulous and corrupt police officials would start pressurising the MLAs to give 'minutes' to the CM in their favour. Soon the legislators learnt that there was money to make in the police postings and the highest bidder would get 'minutes' in his favour.

I have already mentioned about the CM handing over the requests of the legislators to me for further action. This 'role' became a serious headache for me in the later days. I would be bombarded with telephone calls by the legislators and if for any reason I said that their request could not be acceded to, I would be at the receiving end. I had become a bad officer, disliked not only by the ministers and legislators but by my own colleagues. When I learnt that the Home Secretary and the DG and IGP had objected to my 'interference' in police transfers, I was very upset and immediately told the CM that he should directly talk to DG and IGP or the Additional DGP (Administration) rather than asking me to convey his orders. He agreed and for a while, I was relieved of this task. But when his personal staff made blunders in conveying his orders or when they played mischief, I was once again requested to continue doing this 'dirty' work.

This role put me into a lot of difficulties. I recall an incident about the request made by HD Revanna to the CM for transfer of an official. In his usual style the CM had promised the minister that the transfer would be done but didn't pass any orders for the official's transfer. A furious Revanna accosted me and made a caustic remark against me stating that I was not obeying the orders of the CM because I had a vested interest in that matter. Since I felt that his remark cast aspersions on my integrity, I vehemently protested against his unjust remark and told him that I would go rather on leave than hear such remarks. Learning about this incident, Deve Gowda himself spoke to me on phone and placated me.

When a senior Congress legislator and a former minister remarked that I was making money in police transfers, I thought it was the proverbial straw on the camel's back. I firmly told the CM that I shall no longer do any work connected with police transfers. He did agree. For a while, I was free from this task. But the CM would forget that I was no longer doing this task. When he would suddenly telephone me from a remote place in the State and seek details about the transfer of an official, I had to politely remind him that I was no longer doing that task.

An interesting incident needs mention here. On a morning when Principal Secretary SV Ranganath and I were sitting with the CM, he told us that he had received a call from Montek Singh Ahluwalia, Dy Chairman of the Planning Commission, with a request to give an important post to a Punjabi speaking IPS officer. Ranganath noted down the name of the officer and told him that as the transfers of IPS officers was due any time, the request would be considered. The CM was very particular that the officer should be given a 'very prominent' post in Bangalore so as to keep the Dy Chairman in good humour. The officer was given a 'good' post and we all forgot about it.

A few weeks later, I went with the CM to attend the National Development Council meeting in Delhi. As we were entering the meeting hall, I saw Ahluwalia in the lobby. I immediately told the CM to inform Ahluwalia that his request for the IPS officer's transfer had been attended to. Singh very happily went over to Ahluwalia and informed him that his request for transfer had been attended to. The Dy Chairman was taken aback and told the CM that he had never telephoned Singh and he would be the last person to request for any officer's transfer. All of us were flabbergasted. An embarrassed CM asked Ranganath to conduct an enquiry.

On our return to Bangalore, we called the concerned officer and 'grilled' him. He admitted that he had made one of his relatives in Delhi to impersonate as Ahluwalia and call the CM. We wanted to get disciplinary proceedings initiated against the officer but later thought that such a move would further embarrass the CM. The officer was warned and let off!

12

Deputy CM Faces Action from His Party

While the CM was facing internal dissent, things were also not going well in the JD(S) either. Deputy CM Siddaramaiah with his AHINDA programme had become a thorn in the flesh to Deve Gowda who wanted his immediate ouster from the State Cabinet.

On July 24, Siddaramaiah organised 'AHINDA' rally at Hubli to woo minorities and backward classes. It was the first of the four such rallies which had been planned and it was very well attended. What surprised many was that some important Congress and BJP leaders also took part in the rally. It was reported that Deve Gowda was terribly irked over this and that he vowed to take immediate action against the Deputy CM.

On July 28, Deve Gowda phoned the CM and informed him that he would be going to Delhi to meet Sonia Gandhi and that he would ask her

- (i) to take action against all the Congressmen who participated in AHINDA rally at Hubli,
- (ii) to prevent loyalists of SM Krishna from publicly criticising him,
- (iii) to strictly follow the Maharashtra pattern of coalition government,
- (iv) to immediately reconstitute various Boards and Corporations, and

(v) not to think of replacing Dharam Singh as the CM.

He said that he would be willing to partner with Congress at the national level too. The very next day Deve Gowda met Sonia Gandhi, had an hour-long meeting with her in which she had apparently agreed to most of his demands.

I had also learnt that Siddaramaiah would be ousted from the party the same day and that MP Prakash would be made the Deputy CM. I conveyed this information to Singh.

On July 29 I learnt that the JD(S) Legislature Party meeting was to be convened on August 1, and during this meeting, the Deputy CM would be formally shown the door from the party. My source in the JD(S) informed me that they believed that the Congress would admit Siddaramaiah in October and that the coalition would break immediately thereafter. He also informed me that DK Shivakumar had advised Siddaramaiah to tour the State extensively and mobilise the backward classes.

On July 31, the CM spoke to me from Delhi where he had gone to meet his party leaders along with Kharge stating that they had a high-level meeting with the Party president and that there was a consensus about admitting Siddaramaiah into the Congress fold. The same day I learnt that senior leaders of JD(S) MP Prakash and PGR Sindhia pleaded with Deve Gowda not to remove Siddaramaiah from the party but Gowda was unmoved.

On August 1, 52 MLAs and 7 MLCs of the JD(S) met and resolved to remove Siddaramaiah from the leadership of the JDLP. In addition, it was also resolved to take disciplinary action against Dr HC Mahadevappa and Satish Jarkiholi who were close confidants of the Deputy CM. I informed these developments immediately to the CM.

On August 2, the Deputy CM Siddaramaiah called a press conference and stated that the JDLP meeting held the previous day was illegal and that he would continue to champion the cause of AHINDA.

On August 3, Kumaraswamy and 51 other MLAs of JD(S) met and resolved to oust Siddaramaiah from the party. They met the Speaker and the CM and gave them a letter in this regard.

The next day a close confidant of Deve Gowda told me that the JD(S) supremo wanted Siddaramaiah and his associates to be ousted from the Cabinet urgently. When I communicated this news to the CM, he brushed it aside stating that he had just then spoken to Gowda who had told the CM to take his time.

On August 5, I once again conveyed to the CM that Gowda was quite upset that no action had been taken against the Deputy CM and if things got delayed, the JD(S) might withdraw support to the government. I also told him that Deve Gowda wanted the change of portfolios of some of the JD(S) ministers. The CM called a meeting of some leaders of his party to discuss this matter. Kharge, RV Deshpande, HK Patil, and KK Murthy attended.

I was told that the leaders felt that when Deve Gowda was hobnobbing with the BJP, the Congress party should not sack Siddaramaiah in a hurry and that the CM was advised not to immediately give a letter to the Governor for removing the Deputy CM. The leaders had also felt that the letter to the Governor should go only after the Speaker of the Assembly recognised MP Prakash as the leader of the JDLP.

I was told that the CM consulted his Party high command, the Governor, and other experts and at 7.30 PM he went to Raj Bhavan and gave the letter to the Governor asking him to drop the Deputy CM with two others.

Siddaramaiah Finally Sacked

On August 6, 2005, acting on the basis of the CM's letter the Governor relieved Siddaramaiah from the post of Deputy CM. He also relieved two other ministers Dr HC Mahadevappa and Satish Jarkiholi from the Cabinet. Revenue Minister Prakash was appointed the new Deputy CM.

Prakash had earlier worked as a minister under four different Chief Ministers namely, Ramakrishna Hegde, SR Bommai, HD Deve Gowda and JH Patel. He belonged to the powerful Lingayat community. He was known as a man of varied interests, especially in theatre. He spoke well and wrote well. In his hometown of Huvina Hadagali in Bellary district, he would organise a drama festival annually and invite famous troupes from various parts of the State. I had attended one such festival.

BJP also had its share of problems during that period. On August 3, a group of BJP MLAs met at the residence of Yeddyurappa and declared their support to the move of aligning with the JD(S). They are also said to have discussed breaking away from the BJP and to float a new party called Samajwadi Janata Party. This had naturally worried the party leadership.

On August 6, Ved Prakash Goel, BJP observer from Delhi arrived in Bangalore. I was told that Yeddyurappa didn't meet him. I was also told by my sources that Yeddyurappa was planning to split the party as he had been assured of the support of 38 MLAs. These legislators had met in the residence of Anil Lad. They were prepared to do anything to get into power but Deve Gowda had not yet agreed to form a coalition with them.

Fluid Situation

I was also surprised to learn from a source that Yeddyurappa was in touch with the Congress top brass and that he had been told that if he brought 53 MLAs with him, the party was prepared to align with him.

The BJP top brass was worried about these developments and Venkaiah Naidu was being sent to Bangalore to monitor the developments.

On August 7, Yeddyurappa met the media persons at his residence and announced that there was no rift in the BJP and that there was no question of his leaving the party. A journalist who attended the press meet informed me that at Yeddyurappa's residence there was only one Member of Parliament, 14 MLAs and two MLCs in support.

Though every political observer felt that the coalition government would not last long, none knew when the coalition would break.

On August 14, the CM told me that he had information that a JD(S) leader had contacted Shobha Karandlaje, BJP legislator, and was trying for a split in BJP ranks. Three days later the AICC in-charge of Karnataka Antony arrived in Bangalore. I was informed that a large number of dissident Congressmen met him at the Guest House where he was staying and complained against the CM. Antony remained mum over the participation of Congressmen in the AHINDA rally.

The AHINDA rally was held in Tumkur on August 20. RL Jalappa, Congress MP and VS Ugrappa, Congress MLC attended the rally. The speakers at the rally were critical of Deve Gowda and Kumaraswamy for the unceremonious removal of Siddaramaiah from the cabinet.

On August 23, I learnt that Kumaraswamy had met Yeddyurappa and other leaders of the BJP and held long discussions. Meanwhile, a top Congress leader, who had been denied a cabinet berth, told me that a section of his partymen had planned to induct Siddaramaiah into the Congress party which would result in Deve Gowda withdrawing support to the Congress. When the coalition government fell, they would get the assembly dissolved and go for elections. They were planning to project Kharge as the CM candidate and bring back SM Krishna, the then Governor of Maharashtra, as the KPCC President.

As the month of August was coming to a close, the CM was in a fix to name the new DG and IGP because Albuquerque was retiring by the month end. There were only two contenders for the coveted post in the reckoning - BS Sial and KR Srinivasan. Officers close to Sial had told me that he was apprehensive of not getting the post as he had been away from Karnataka for a long time which might be held against him. The posting of KR Srinivasan earlier as in-charge DGP CID, even when he had held the rank of Addl DGP, was cited as a reason for this apprehension. Another apprehension was about the role I might play as the Chief of Intelligence.

It was indeed a fact that KR Srinivasan who had started his career as Asst Superintendent of Police in Yadgir in Gulbarga district had known Dharam Singh since the early seventies. The taluk of Jewargi to which the CM belonged to, came under the jurisdiction of ASP Yadgir then. Besides, he was very close to many political bigwigs across party ranks. He was a darling of police officers of all ranks.

I had started my career as an Asst Superintendent of Police under KR Srinivasan and was perceived to be very close to him. Many of my colleagues had thought that as I had the ears of the CM, I might probably suggest the name of Srinivasan for the post of DG and IGP. I suspect that these colleagues might have poisoned the mind of Sial against me.

I, however, knew how the mind of Dharam Singh worked. Sial, apart from being the senior-most officer in the State, was a Sikh officer. I knew that when the Prime Minister of the country was a Sikh, the CM would never think of overlooking Sial. The CM neither sought my opinion, nor did I volunteer to give it while making this appointment. As expected by me, on the evening of August 30th, Sial was appointed as the new DG and IGP of Karnataka. When I called on Sial to congratulate him on his elevation, he was quite cold to me. At once I realised that our relations would not have a smooth sail henceforth.

On September 22, 2005, Siddaramaiah was suspended from the JD(S). Meanwhile, the relation between the CM and Deve Gowda had soured. It was rumoured that Gowda had met SM Krishna and had spoken to him about replacing the CM. While I didn't believe this report, I figured that it was a ploy by the JD(S) to make the Congress listen to its demands. Five days later, I learnt that Gowda had told people close to him that he would not hesitate to join hands with the BJP and run the government. At that time I didn't know that his words would become prophetic.

The political situation had become quite fluid. While those Congressmen who had become ministers or those who had got some plum positions wanted the coalition to continue, those deprived of power wanted the coalition to break and go for elections. They thought that by admitting Siddaramaiah to the Congress party, their chances of getting a majority in elections were bright. They reckoned that Siddaramaiah would be able to get a large number of voters from Kuruba and other backward classes to vote for the Congress.

Just as the relationship between the Congress and JD(S) was strained, the relationship between Sial, DG and IGP and me was under stress though he had assumed office only a month ago. He kept on finding faults with everything I did and bombarded me with advisory memos almost every day. He was under the impression that I was not sharing with him all the information which I was giving to the CM. This was not a fact. All matters concerning the security of the State and law and order were promptly shared with him as I had done with the three DGPs who had preceded him. On October 1, when I attended a meeting in his office to discuss arrangements to be made for the Police Martyrs Day, he expressed in front of all the senior police officers present that he would not like to see my face. I replied to him that he was welcome to get me transferred out if he so desired.

On October 8, I learnt that Gowda was very angry with the CM regarding posting of some key officials, and appointment of chiefs of Boards and Corporations. I was told that the former PM wanted the cabinet to be reshuffled before the Zilla Panchayat/Taluk Panchayat elections. He also was planning to present a chargesheet against Dharam Singh to Sonia Gandhi listing Singh's shortcomings as a CM. I promptly conveyed this news to the CM. Surprisingly the CM was not perturbed by hearing this news. He had attended an assessment meeting of Congress Chief Ministers at Chandigarh on the previous day where the party leaders had complimented him for some of the developmental initiatives taken in the State. Singh told me that Gowda's demands could not be immediately met and that he would wait and see.

An issue which worried all the three major political parties at that time was the holding of elections to the Zilla/Taluk Panchayats (ZP/TP). Consequent to a ruling by the Supreme Court, the elections had to be held within six weeks of the court order. But no party was interested in the elections. Efforts were, therefore, made to persuade MR Hegde, the then State Election Commissioner, to get the elections postponed under some pretext. Hegde stuck to his guns of following the court order. Being the former Law Secretary of the State, he didn't want to risk contempt of court. Hence, he announced the election dates on 14th October.

HDD Hounds NRN

Around the same time, Deve Gowda targeted his *bête noire* SM Krishna in two different ways. Using a World Bank report, "India Investment Climate Assessment 2004", which stated that Karnataka was among the most corrupt States in India, he tried to portray that during the tenure of Krishna as the Chief Minister, the State was perceived to be very corrupt.

Secondly, he targeted those Information Technology/ Biotechnology stalwarts such as NR Narayana Murthy of Infosys who were considered to be close to Krishna. After attending a presentation on 'Shifting focus on Urban-Rural Partnership' made by NR Narayana Murthy, Gowda told the media that while he was not against the IT sector as perceived, he would not allow large chunks of land to be given to IT companies. He attacked the Bangalore Agenda Task Force (BATF) which had been constituted during the time of Krishna saying that BATF was an initiative that failed to deliver its promise. In a letter to CM Dharam Singh, he attacked Narayana Murthy stating that Murthy had not contributed much for the development of Bangalore International Airport of which he (Murthy) was the Chairman.

The reactions to Gowda's utterances came quick. Krishna hit back saying that corruption was more rampant when Gowda was the State CM. He also reacted to the statement by Dharam Singh that the government would order an enquiry 'if need be' on the findings in the report, by stating that such a probe should begin with the Public Works Department. Everyone was aware that Dharam Singh was the PWD Minister when Krishna was the CM.

Krishna didn't take the matter lying down. His Secretary in the Mumbai Raj Bhavan, Jayakar Jerome, sought clarification on the report by the World Bank and the Bank replied to Jerome stating that there was nothing in its study to claim that Karnataka was the most corrupt State in 2004.

A hurt Narayana Murthy sent in his resignation from the post of Chairman, Bangalore International Airport Limited (BIAL) with effect from October 20. In a letter to Singh, he said that he was pained that none clarified his role in BIAL and the work he had so far done.

Dharam Singh was quite upset by all these developments. He was also worried about the growing dissidence within his own party. On the morning of October 31, when the two of us were sipping tea, he told me that he could become the Chief Minister only due to his good nature and support of Deve Gowda. He said that though he had won three bye-elections as KPCC president, he had been asked to resign from the post by Ghulam Nabi Azad and as a loyal soldier of the party he had complied without a murmur. He stated that though many senior leaders in the party had gone against Indira Gandhi, he had remained steadfast and was loyal to the party and the Gandhi family. When asked which senior Congress leader had supported him to become the Chief Minister, he revealed the name of Pranab Mukherjee.

He stated that many senior Congressmen were not very happy that he had become the Chief Minister and were working overtime to unseat him. He revealed that his own party men had worked against the official Congress candidate in the Shimoga

Lok Sabha bye-election little knowing that with Bangarappa's victory the Congress party itself had become shaky within Karnataka. He said that his party men had thought that if the Congress candidate won the Shimoga bye-election, he (Singh) would become stronger and that was the reason for the sabotage. He also felt that KK Murthy was not selected to contest Legislative Council elections only to spite him.

Over a period of time, the CM had developed considerable trust in me and used to consider me as a member of his family rather than a government officer. He had watched me for many decades. I was a trainee IPS officer in Gulbarga district in 1978 when he first became a minister. I was the Superintendent of Police in Bidar district when he continued in Gundu Rao's Cabinet. When he was the Home Minister in the cabinet of Bangarappa, I was the Deputy Inspector General of Police of the Gulbarga Range.

After I became the Head of Intelligence under him, he would treat me as a confidante and confide many things with me. While the relationship between me and Krishna was more formal, between me and Singh it was very informal. When my father passed away, Singh came to my residence to pay his last respects. This was an unusual gesture on the part of any CM and I was quite touched.

Apart from Dharam Singh, everyone in his family considered me as their own. I have lost count how many times I had breakfast or a meal with the CM in his house. I never exploited my proximity with Dharam Singh for my personal gains. Right from the day I joined IPS, it had been drilled in my mind that I was answerable only to the Constitution of India and none else. I never gave any advice to any CM which I thought was administratively wrong. I have been over-ruled many times but I have done my duty. I can very confidently claim that I was more loyal to my office than to the CM. Being a very seasoned politician, Dharam Singh understood this and never gave me a task which would embarrass an officer or which an officer was not expected to do.

There have been many similarly placed officers who have used their proximity to the powers that be for their personal advancement. Many officers who have worked in the Intelligence Wing have joined politics. Many have received post-retirement sinecures. I had no such desires. I have already recounted how I politely refused the offer of becoming the Police Commissioner of Bangalore city twice earlier. That missed chance never came my way again, but I have no regrets. I feel that because of my stint in the Intelligence with the Congress Chief Ministers, I was denied the post of Head of the Police Department. I shall recount that incident later.

What type of person was Dharam Singh? In his dress, he was not fussy. Most of the time one would find him wearing white cotton 'Pyjama-Kurta'. Sometimes he would wear a 'Nehru Jacket'. It was very rare to see him wear a lounge suit. In food, he was quite frugal. He liked to have the typical Gulbarga food of Jowar Rottis and its usual accompaniments of different types of chutney. Unlike people of Gulbarga, he wouldn't eat spicy food. At home, his wife Prabhavathi Dharam Singh used to personally serve him food. Though he used to like non-vegetarian food, he had drastically reduced eating it. Though he liked sweets, he used to consume them less. But he liked to drink quite often the sugary tea which people in Gulbarga love.

Talking about tea served in Gulbarga, a joke I had heard as a probationer comes to mind. It used to be said that the number of spoons of sugar that a host mixes in the cup of tea offered to a guest is directly proportional to the standing the guest has in society. While a clerk would have two spoons of sugar in his tea, a District Collector would get four and a Minister six.

When he used to be in good mood, Dharam Singh would hum songs from old Hindi movies. He was very proficient in Urdu poetry and was very fond of Ghazals. He was fond of quoting a particular couplet, *"Dil mile ya na mile, kum se kum haath milate rahe"* (loosely translated it means "even if we don't touch each other's hearts, let us at least keep holding hands"). This couplet mirrors his personality.

He was so fond of Urdu poetry, he would organise Mushaira meets in Bidar and Gulbarga. As the CM he attended the International Urdu Conference at Bangalore and seeing the galaxy of foreign poets he recited a couplet "*Woh aye the hamare ghar khuda ke tarah, hum kabhi ghar ko, kabhi unko dekhte rahe*" (they visited my abode, like Gods from above; I kept looking in disbelief, once at them and once at my abode).

Unlike SM Krishna, he was not fond of serious reading. He was fond of cricket and would follow test and IPL matches when time permitted. Like Krishna, he had a few steadfast friends. They were Kulkarni, Dharam Vir and Harinder Singh, all living in Hyderabad. The first two worked with Government of India in different capacities. I have seen the three friends meet often and enjoy their time together reciting Urdu poetry.

Though politics would consume most of his time, he liked to spend quality time with his children and grandchildren. Many people are not aware that Singh named his daughter Priyadarshini after Indira Gandhi. Whenever he came from long tours Dharam Singh would look for his grandchildren, hug them and spend at least a few minutes with them before doing anything else.

Singh could speak many languages with ease. Apart from Hindi, Kannada, and Urdu which he could read and write, he could speak in Marathi and Telugu too.

A special trait of Dharam Singh needs mention here. Before leaving home on any work, he would invariably take the blessings of the womenfolk present at home. He also showed great respect for elders and treated his elder sister-in-law as his mother.

Singh would rarely display anger with any officers, more so with those who were close to him. When he became angry, he would bite his tongue and we would know that he was upset. Once I was travelling with him in his car from the airport to his residence. I was in the front seat and he was sitting in the back with his wife. Vincent George, Secretary to Sonia Gandhi, had tried to contact him through his OSD Krishnaiah. As the OSD was travelling in another car, he gave George my cell number saying that the CM could be contacted through my phone. When I got the call, I passed on my phone to the CM. While receiving the phone from my hand, the handset slipped down and the connection was lost. Singh lost his cool and started shouting at me. His wife pacified him stating that it was not my fault. That was the second time he got angry with me which was unwarranted.

The third and the only other time I faced his wrath was when Ghulam Nabi Azad came to Bangalore on July 30, 2005. On that evening when I had come back home from work, Dharam Singh called me on my cell phone and in an angry tone asked me to go on leave. Totally taken aback, I asked him the reason for his order. He passed on the phone to his assistant who told me that the CM was upset because we had not provided Azad with a pilot and escort vehicle. On enquiry with my officers, I learnt that Azad had indeed been provided with an escort and as his security classification did not require a pilot vehicle, the same had not been provided.

Before I could give my explanation to the CM, he had already left for Delhi with Azad and Mallikarjuna Kharge. When I spoke to him on the phone in the night, he had cooled down and was his usual self. That was Dharam Singh. He could never be angry with anyone for long.

After the resignation of Narayana Murthy from BIAL, there was a lot of criticism against the government in the media. Narayana Murthy was very close to the Prime Minister, Planning Commission Dy Chairman Montek Singh Ahluwalia and others. His resignation had brought out into sharp focus the fault lines of the coalition government. Singh tried to make amends by inviting Murthy to his residence for a breakfast meeting. I was told Murthy had breakfast with the CM, but politely declined to reconsider withdrawal of his resignation from BIAL.

Auto-Pilot Mode

On November 17, *Kannada Prabha,* a Kannada daily from Bangalore, published a survey report about the mood of the people of Karnataka. It mentioned that the people of the State were fed up with the performance of the government and wanted mid-term elections to be held.

As a matter of fact, I agreed with the findings of the survey. The government appeared to be running on auto-pilot mode as both the parties were more interested in politics rather than administration. JD(S) party leaders were spending more time in transfers of officials and about the next move of Siddaramaiah rather than governance. The party was trying to woo important leaders of the powerful Lingayat community into its fold.

The Congress party was riddled with dissensions and many leaders were openly showing their discomfort with the coalition partner and thinking of ways and means of getting out of the coalition. What was common among both the parties was their mutual worry about the outcome of the impending Zilla Panchayat/Taluk Panchayat elections as they were aware that the results of elections would be a pointer to the mood of the electorate. Administration of the State was the last thought in anyone's mind.

Around this time, the CM asked me to make a quick assessment of the outcome of Zilla Panchayat polls. I took about ten days to get the surveys done. When I reported that in about fourteen districts, the Congress would get a majority, he felt supremely happy. I mentioned to him that in the coastal districts of Karnataka, a majority of Hindus had turned away from the Congress. He was not surprised by this information.

On November 24, the CM and Deve Gowda had a one-on-one meeting in the residence of KK Murthy. I learnt that the main topic of discussion was the entry of Siddaramaiah to the Congress party. Though Dharam Singh was under pressure to oppose to Siddaramaiah's entry, Congress leaders such as Oscar

Fernandes, Veerappa Moily, RL Jalappa, and Mallikarjuna Kharge had reportedly met AK Antony, AICC observer for Karnataka, and pressed for Siddaramaiah's admission to the party. During the one-on-one meeting, Deve Gowda reportedly told the CM that the government would collapse if the Congress admitted Siddaramaiah.

At this point in time, I was under tremendous stress. I had to be on my toes always and be aware of what was happening around. Apart from calls from legislators, I had to be available for answering queries by Deve Gowda or his party leaders. As Singh would be busy with other duties, I used to be called by all and sundry. I used to work almost for fifteen to sixteen hours every day and had no time for my family.

The attitude of DG and IGP Sial towards me had added to my woes. I felt that though I continued to meet him regularly and apprise him of all the important events that were happening in the State, he nursed a grievance against me. Many of my colleagues in the IPS would tell me that during meetings, he would openly criticise me. I met Sial several times and tried to clarify my position but it appeared to me that he didn't believe me. The DG and IGP continued to bombard me with memos, apart from seeking urgent reports on matters which I thought were not serious. Fortunately, the officers working with me, especially Auradkar, DIG, shared a lot of my burden.

The elections to Zilla Panchayats/Taluk Panchayats were held on December 19 and the polling percentage was 70. The results which were out ten days later surprised everyone. The Congress had bagged almost 490 seats out of 1,005 in ZPs and 170 out of 3,657 in taluk Panchayats. This meant that the Congress could effectively control 14 of the 27 ZPs. The JD(S) bagged about 270 ZP seats getting control of two ZPs and the BJP secured 152 seats. No party got a majority in 11 Zilla Panchayats. The CM communicated this news to his party chief who appeared to be very happy with the performance of her party.

Terrorist Attack at IISc Campus

The jubilation on the morning of December 28 soon turned tragic that evening. At about 5 PM, I received the news that terrorists had struck the campus of Indian Institute of Science in Bangalore killing a scientist. I rushed to CM's office and gave him this shocking news. Later both of us drove together to the IISc campus and visited the scene of offence. A terrorist had reportedly fired on a group of scientists attending a seminar with his AK-47 rifle indiscriminately killing a scientist MC Puri and injuring five others. Apart from indulging in firing, the terrorists had also lobbed hand grenades. This was probably the very first terrorist attack in Bangalore and it shook everyone.

On visiting the scene of the tragedy, I felt a sense of guilt that my department had not anticipated the terrorist strike and had not alerted the concerned to take preventive measures. I consoled myself that as the attack was masterminded from across the border the various Central Intelligence agencies should have collected such information and shared their inputs with us. In the instant case, even the Central agencies had no specific clue about the IISc attack.

I kept thinking whether it is possible for the Intelligence agencies to predict and prevent any unfortunate event. My seniors told me that despite all efforts to prevent any untoward event, such incidents take place. They stated that while the Intelligence and security agencies succeed in preventing 80% of terrorist-related incidents, 20% do happen despite all precautions by the police. They cited the classic example of the attack on the World Trade Centre in New York in support of their contention. An all-powerful nation like the United States with so much of resources at its command could not predict and prevent the 9/11 incident, though the World Trade Centre had earlier been subjected to bombing. They comforted me by saying that despite so many drawbacks like lack of trained and motivated manpower, lack of technical gadgets we had managed well.

A senior IAS officer on coming to know about my dejection cheered me by mentioning that due to timely inputs not a single serious law and order incident had taken place during Dharam Singh's tenure. He mentioned that when Singh claimed during the Congress Chief Ministers' conference that no police firing had taken place in the State in the past two years, every one present expressed surprise. He also stated that we had done fairly well in preventing the spread of Naxalite activities in Karnataka.

While reflecting about the years that had gone by, I was surprised to note that while the year 2004 had ended with Tsunami tragedy, the year 2005 had ended with the terrorist attack. I looked forward to the coming year with hope.

13

VIP Security

VIP Security was one of the major duties performed by the Intelligence Wing I headed. While the security of the Chief Minister was the primary responsibility of the police which had jurisdiction of the place where he/she was present at any given moment, the coordination of this work with different police units was taken care of by the State Intelligence.

For instance, if the CM went to Gulbarga, the security during his/her stay at Gulbarga was to be taken care of by the SP, Gulbarga district whereas security in Bangalore was to be taken care of by the City Police Commissioner. The VIP Security Branch of the State Intelligence would coordinate with the CM's office and circulate the CM's tour programmes to all concerned police officials and would generally supervise the security work.

A book of instructions called the 'Yellow Book' had been prepared by the State Intelligence to help police officials in various districts and cities in Karnataka to plan the security of the CM during his visits and stay in their jurisdiction. This was similar to the 'Blue Book' designed for the Prime Minister's security. We had a big contingent of officers and men headed by an officer of the rank of Superintendent of Police to take care of the Chief Minister's proximate security. Wherever the CM travelled, we sent our protection teams in advance and also with him to give him ring round protection.

While the jurisdictional police were required to take full responsibility for the security of any visiting dignitary, the

State Intelligence was meant to help them in planning and organising security for VIPs during public functions, meetings, journeys by road and train etc. The State Intelligence was to provide Intelligence inputs about threats to VIP Security in advance to the local police. The State Intelligence Unit also provided a Security Liaison Officer to the visiting VIPs like Union Ministers, foreign heads of State/Government and any other person who was given categorised security.

The State Intelligence liaised with the Central security agencies like the Special Protection Group which was concerned with the proximate security of the Prime Minister and the Intelligence Bureau which took care of VIP Security. It also liaised with Bureau of Security of the Central Government and the Central Industrial Security Force in respect of airport security, the Railway Protection Force in respect of railways etc. The question of providing personal security officers (bodyguards in common parlance) to various people depended entirely on the State Intelligence.

I headed the Security Categorisation Committee of Karnataka State which would periodically assess the threat perception of important personages and decide on the scale of protection a person was entitled to, like Z plus, Z, X, and Y category of security. In simple terms, the Committee was to determine how many security men a VIP should have with him round the clock. A number of reports would be sought from various agencies to assess the threat perception of an individual. I also headed another committee which would decide on providing 'gunmen' to various individuals including Ministers.

It is a common perception that security goes hand in hand with a person's position. Constitutional authorities like the President, the Vice-President, the Prime Minister, the Governor of a State and important personages like the Chief Minister have to be provided security because anything untoward happening to them will reflect very badly on the entire nation. For others, providing security purely goes by the threat they face. Whether an individual who does not occupy any position in the government should be provided security by the State is a point that can be debated *ad nauseum*. If the State provided security to a private individual, should such an individual pay for the service provided is also a matter that needs consideration. There cannot be a hard and fast rule regarding providing security to an individual and every case needs to be considered separately.

Some years ago many persons who considered that they are important clamoured to have a gunman to move around as it was considered a status symbol. We already had a list of over one hundred protectees in the State and I was under constant pressure to add to this list. However, I succeeded in warding off many requests at the cost of being 'unpopular'. I also downgraded the security details of many individuals during my time.

It must be mentioned here that no one can be provided 'fool-proof' or 'fail-proof' security. During my training for the VIP Security duties for the Non-Aligned Meeting in Delhi, I had been told that while the would-be assassin has to be lucky only once, a security man has to be lucky all the time in his effort to protect his 'charge'. History is replete with instances wherein highly protected Presidents and Prime Ministers have been assassinated or kidnapped. To cite an instance in Karnataka, while matinee idol Dr Rajkumar, who had not been given security from the government, was kidnapped by Veerappan, former minister H Nagappa was abducted and killed by the same forest brigand despite being provided with a gunman. I would cite this instance whenever pressure was mounted from people to provide them Personal Security Officers.

One of the persons who constantly pressured me to provide him with security was the late politician S Ramesh, who was referred often as 'Slum' Ramesh. He was a very close friend of Kumaraswamy. Both of them were dabbling in film production. Ramesh was no doubt under a life threat, but it was because of some financiers who had lent him money for film production. He was quite close to me because of his timely inputs about what was happening in the JD(S). Still I could not provide him with any categorised security because rules prevented it. When Dharam Singh had asked me to reconsider my decision, I had to politely tell him that it was not possible as it would open floodgates of such requests.

According to the rules, the Categorisation Committee could decide whether an individual should pay for the security provided or otherwise. A majority of the applicants wanted the State to provide security free of cost, but a good number of individuals were willing to pay any amount to get a policeman to go around with them as gunman. It was not unusual to get applications for security from underworld dons, rowdies, and such other undesirable elements. The committee had to, therefore, consider each request very carefully.

Amusing Factor

What used to amuse me during that time were the constant requests by Swamijis of various mathas to provide them with police security. The personal secretary of the Swamiji of a prominent matha used to pester me with requests to grant an escort party to the Swamiji, who had already been given a Personal Security Officer. In order to ward him off, I told him that the cost of security and the fuel for the jeep provided has to be borne by the matha. He unhesitatingly agreed. When I asked him why a person who has renounced worldly things should fear for his life and demand police protection, with a sheepish smile he said the Swamiji during his tours would have to carry lots of costly ornaments belonging to the matha and hence the request for a police escort. He also pointed out that the Swamiji of another matha in the neighbouring district had been given a police escort, and his Swamiji should also be treated likewise and get similar 'facility'.

During my tenure in the Intelligence Wing, I rejected requests of many Swamijis which made me unpopular among the followers of various mathas, including ministers and bureaucrats. My colleagues used to jocularly say that I would be subjected to innumerable curses from the mathas for my refusal to oblige them and might face their wrath in future.

Those days, we had inputs that the software companies in Bangalore, especially Infosys, would be a target of terrorist attack. A rough sketch map about the location of the Infosys campus in Electronic City in the outskirts of Bangalore had been recovered from a suspected terrorist. We were naturally worried and alerted Infosys to beef up its security. Meanwhile, we decided to provide personal security to Narayana Murthy. I wrote a letter to him informing our decision. He politely refused to have any PSO from the government. Later on, I sent the SP in-charge of Security to meet him and persuade him to have police protection. He did not budge. He is probably the one and the only person who refused our security. It is not out of place to mention here that Vijay Mallya and several other businessmen and industrialists demanded security from the government and there was a clamour from our personnel to work with such 'VIPs' for the various perks that would ensue.

I have already mentioned my interactions with Indira Gandhi during my tenure as SP, Intelligence earlier. During my tenure as ADG Intelligence, I had to make security arrangements for many dignitaries who visited Bangalore.

Among those who visited the State during that time were the President of India, Dr Abdul Kalam, Prime Ministers Dr Manmohan Singh, and Atal Bihari Vajpayee, the then CM of Gujarat Narendra Modi, the President of Senegal Abdoulaye Wade, etc. Whenever the Prime Minister visited the State it was incumbent on the State Police Chief to be present at all places visited by the PM and supervise the security arrangements. Over a period of time, this role was delegated to the Head of Intelligence. The DG and IGP used to receive and see off the PM at the airport and would not generally go with the PM whenever he travelled outside the State Headquarters.

Within a month of my taking over the post of ADG Intelligence, Prime Minister Vajpayee came to Bangalore on

May 3, 2003. Ever since my college days, I had admired PM Vajpayee for his oratorical skills. I liked his down-to-earth approach to life and his love for poetry. During that visit, he participated in a function in the HAL airport and saw the aerial display of the indigenously built light combat aircraft. He named the aircraft as Tejas. I thought this was the most appropriate name and only a poet like our PM could think of such a name.

My next meeting with Atal Bihari Vajpayee was during his visit to Belgaum. This was during an election rally in May 2004. I noticed that during this rally the PM did not speak as effectively as he would earlier speak. I thought age had caught up with him.

Because of his knee surgery, Atal Bihari Vajpayee had considerable trouble in moving about. I had noticed that he would avoid climbing stairs. Whenever he had to board his special aircraft, he would use the ambu-lift.

Prime Minister Dr Manmohan Singh visited Karnataka once during my tenure as ADG, Intelligence. A mention has already been made about his visit immediately after the killing of policemen in Venkatammanahalli. During this visit, he visited Mysore to inaugurate the Corporate Training Centre of Infosys in Mysore. He also visited Suttur Math to inaugurate a building called Dasoha Bhavana.

I accompanied the PM sitting in his escort helicopter. During this visit, I noticed that he was quite friendly with Narayana Murthy and Mrs Sudha Murthy. I was told that Montek Singh Ahluwalia and Murthy were good friends and Ahluwalia was responsible for getting the PM to agree to go to Mysore and inaugurate the Infosys facility.

Dr Abdul Kalam, the President of India, visited our State a couple of times during those days. Like the PM, he also visited Suttur Math in Mysore but what I remember about his Mysore visit was his interaction with school children. Like a typical teacher, he conducted that interactive session. I was surprised by his love and affection towards the younger generation.

Everyone is aware of how simple and humble Dr Kalam was. He had absolutely no airs and was always smiling. He was truly the people's President. I remember that during a couple of his visits, a white haired-white bearded gentleman would accompany him in the Presidential aircraft. Out of curiosity, I made enquiries about this gentleman. I was told that he was Dr YS Rajan, a former colleague of the President at ISRO and his close friend. He had co-authored *India 2020: A Vision for the New Millennium* with the President of India Dr APJ Abdul Kalam.

In one of Dr Kalam's visits to Bangalore, during a road journey, he stopped his convoy and suddenly got down from his car in Gurappanapalya (a very congested locality in South Bangalore) and began walking. The escorting policemen were taken aback and followed him. He entered a house and came back after a few minutes. Monitoring his movements sitting in my office, I was on tenterhooks. I was later informed that he had visited an ailing friend. Though the President was least bothered about protocol or security, his action did carry a security risk.

Occupying a high office had not changed his personality at all. Dr Kalam would always display so much zeal and enthusiasm I would envy his boundless energy. Age had not caught up with him and those police personnel giving him security coverage would have a hard time catching up with him.

Narendra Modi and Security

Narendra Modi visited the State many times during the Assembly elections in 2004. As he was in Z Plus category security, we had to provide him with bulletproof cars during his visits. Those days only a very few bullet cars were available in the State. And those cars were not having adequate power to move at high speeds because they were built on the platforms of the available cars. Many a time they would develop some mechanical problem or the other. Many dignitaries didn't like to use these cars, but we had to insist that they make use of the cars in the interest of their own safety.

During CM Narendra Modi's visit to Karnataka, his own security team from Gujarat provided him with close protection and I had to interact with the Gujarat Police during such visits. Like our President, Modi used to be indefatigable. He travelled long distances by road to address election meetings.

Sonia Gandhi visited the State a couple of times. She was protected by the SPG as she had a serious security threat. While I didn't personally supervise security arrangements for most of her visits, I didn't want to take chances for her proposed visit to a school run by JSS institutions in Ramapura of Chamarajanagar district. This was because Ramapura was in the Veerappan territory, and the forest brigand was then still at large. I also supervised arrangements for her visit to Dakshina Kannada in April 2004.

Deve Gowda, being the former Prime Minister, was also protected by Special Protection Group. I had then noticed that SPG officials who were posted to guard him were not as efficient as those around Sonia Gandhi. Once I asked an SPG officer the reason for the same and he jokingly stated that Gowda didn't face any security threat. Later on, I was told that consequent to the amendment to the SPG Act, SPG protection to Gowda was withdrawn.

A number of heads of State and heads of governments of other countries also visited Bangalore during those days and I had to interact with the Intelligence Bureau and organise the security of such dignitaries. I remember the Chinese Premier Wen Jiabao's visit to Bangalore in April 2005 very distinctly. We had been warned by the Intelligence Bureau that during his visits some Tibetans would organise protests and that such protesters should be kept under check. I had been given the names of the leaders who would organise such protests. This was communicated to the Commissioner of Police, Bangalore with a request to prevent any untoward incident during the visit of the Chinese Prime Minister.

On the afternoon of April 10, I learnt that when the Chinese PM was visiting the campus of Indian Institute of Science,

Bangalore, a protester who had scaled the central tower of the heritage building displayed a banner on which was written 'Free Tibet'. He also shouted slogans and threw a bunch of pamphlets on the visiting PM. This sudden incident unnerved not only Jiabao but everyone else. If the youth had shot at the visiting PM or hurled a missile and hurt the Chinese supremo, there would have been very serious diplomatic repercussions between the two countries. It could even have lead to a war between our two countries. Fortunately, the youth, who gave his name as Tenzing Tsundue, had only pamphlets in his possession. The youth was overpowered by the police and the visit of the PM to IISc went off smoothly.

On learning about the incident, I rushed to IISc, and conducted a spot inspection and came to the conclusion that there was a serious security lapse on the part of the Bangalore city police. When the police had taken over the building 24 hours prior to the visit and sanitised it, how could a person enter the building was an enigma. It was later learnt that the protester had hidden behind the stairway even before the police took possession of the building. An enquiry about this lapse was ordered by the government and a senior officer almost lost his chance of getting his/her promotion because of this incident.

Another incident involved a foreign dignitary from West Africa. After a ceremonial reception at the airport, he was taken to a five-star hotel for his stay. After midnight I received a call from one of our officers that the dignitary was found missing from his hotel room. I asked him to contact and alert the Security Chief of the visiting delegation who was staying in the same hotel. The visiting delegation only spoke French and we didn't have any French knowing officer. The matter was explained to the Security Chief of the visiting dignitary by sign language. He seemed to understand what had happened but didn't show any surprise about the missing VIP. All our officers were very tense and some of them went on a wild goose chase all around Bangalore. But all their efforts went in vain. Finally, the VIP returned in a private vehicle to the hotel early in the morning and gave a wink to the nervous local police and returned to his room as though nothing had happened.

During all the VIP/VVIP visits to the State, we had to make the security arrangements in consultation with the Central agencies. Fortunately for me, I had excellent contacts with the officials of the Intelligence Bureau (IB) and Special Protection Group (SPG), the two agencies closely involved in security duties of VIP/VVIP. The representatives of the IB in Bangalore those days were Neelamani Raju of my own cadre and Gokulchandran of Maharashtra cadre. Both these officers were very helpful and co-operative and hence, we didn't have to face any problem. I also used to be in touch with the then Special Director of IB ESL Narasimhan (he later became the Governor of Andhra Pradesh) who used to give us timely inputs. In the SPG, my batch-mate and friend BV Wanchoo had occupied a very important position (he too later became the Lt Governor of Goa) and hence it was easy for me to work in coordination with him.

Barring the incident involving the Chinese Prime Minister, all other VVIP and VIP visits to the State concluded without any serious problem and providence had to be thanked for being merciful on the State police. As Douglas McArthur said, "there is no security on this earth, only opportunity."

14

Growing Tensions Within the Congress Party

On the New Year's Day, 2006, when I was at the residence of the CM, I saw HD Kumaraswamy along with a number of JD(S) leaders waiting for the CM to convey their New Year greetings. I drew them into a conversation and asked them about the media reports hinting about the change of government. Kumaraswamy laughed it off and cleverly changed the subject to tell me to be prepared to occupy the post of Police Commissioner, Bangalore shortly. As the CM arrived in the hall at that point in time, I could not continue my conversation with him.

When I met the CM in private later that day, I informed him about the meeting between Krishna and Kharge the previous day. SM Krishna had reached Bangalore on December 30, 2005 and that on December 31, Kharge had met him along with some partymen from Tumkur district. I told the CM that there was a speculation that the two leaders wanted the Congress party to forge an alliance with the AIPJD (All India Progressive Janata Dal). There were reports that the supporters of SM Krishna were planning to exert pressure on the Congress high command to replace Dharam Singh and bring in Kharge as the CM.

The CM was aware that when the coalition government was formed in the State, the name of Kharge was also under active consideration and that Kharge was naturally quite disappointed in not getting the coveted post. Dharam Singh was also aware that ever since he pipped Krishna for the coveted post of the CM, their relationship was under strain. The mutual dislike between Deve Gowda and Krishna was well-known in the State and as the former PM had supported Singh, it was presumed that Krishna would not be fond of Dharam Singh.

Singh had told me on more than one occasion that Krishna would be quite uncomfortable in the Mumbai Raj Bhavan and had predicted that Krishna would not stay there long as a Governor and would be accommodated in the Union Cabinet. This came true later.

Dharam Singh and Deve Gowda Unnerved

Insofar as alignment with the AIPJD party of Siddaramaiah or admitting the former Deputy CM to the Congress party, many Congress leaders had argued that Siddaramaiah's entry into the Congress would bring the backward classes and the minorities to the Congress fold. This, according to them, would help the party get a clear majority in the elections which were bound to be held as the coalition government would collapse.

Suspecting that Siddaramaiah's exit from the JD(S) would diminish its voter base, Deve Gowda had succeeded in admitting many top Lingayat leaders to his party as a counter measure. In fact, his decision to replace Siddaramaiah with MP Prakash, a Lingayat leader later, was probably to gain the support of the powerful community and wean them away from the BJP.

At that time it appeared that Dharam Singh was having little support from his partymen in Karnataka. His survival as the CM was solely dependent on the support of the Congress high command and Deve Gowda. Hence he had tried to keep both in good humour and had largely succeeded till then. As the Congress candidates had fared very well in the Zilla Panchayat elections, he looked forward to continued support from the high command.

On January 2, 2006 I reported to the CM that HD Deve Gowda had stated that there was no question of change of leadership and that the speculative reports in the newspapers that day about SM Krishna and other leaders trying to force the AICC to replace Dharam Singh with Kharge had no basis. Gowda later spoke to the CM from Delhi and I was told that he had reiterated that there would be no change in the government.

On January 3, the direction in which the political winds would blow became apparent to me. In the Zilla Panchayats of Mysore and Mandya, no party had got an absolute majority and a coalition was called for. Both these districts, which had a dominance of the Vokkaliga community, were perceived to be the bastions of the JD(S). A problem arose to the CM when the newly elected Panchayat members having allegiance to the Congress party decided that they would have an alliance with the AIPJD and not the JD(S). They had threatened that they would resign *en masse* if either the Karnataka Pradesh Congress Committee or the AICC forced them to join with the JD(S). To rub salt on the wound, even in the CM's home district of Gulbarga, the Congress ZP members decided to go with the group having allegiance to Siddaramaiah. This unnerved Deve Gowda and he met Ahmed Patel, political secretary of Sonia Gandhi, in Delhi and held discussions to find a way out.

Even though Kumaraswamy had denied only two days earlier about his reported confabulations with BJP leaders, I learnt from unimpeachable sources on the 3rd January that Kumaraswamy was planning to join hands with BJP and had talks with Yeddyurappa. I was informed that Yeddyurappa had told the JD(S) leader that the BJP would consider giving outside support to JD(S) if it was to form the government in the State.

I communicated this news to the CM immediately. He looked terribly worried. In my presence, he spoke to Gowda who was in Delhi. Gowda asserted that he had met Ahmed Patel already and both of them had agreed that the coalition at the State-level would continue without a hitch. He also informed the CM that he was told that the dissidents in the Congress were pressurising the high command to part ways with the JD(S), but the high command was reluctant to do so.

To counter the dissidents, supporters of the CM prepared a presentation to be given to the Congress high command. I had a chance to see it. The spectacular wins in Bidar Lok Sabha, Zilla Panchayat, Taluk Panchayat, and Agriculture Produce Marketing Committee elections were touted as the achievements of Singh.

The CM, however, was worried. Only a day earlier an astrologer had predicted in a newspaper that the days of Singh were numbered. I must mention here that Singh had a great faith in saints, godmen, and astrologers. I have already made a mention of Dwarkanath, a close confidante of Vilasrao Deshmukh and DK Shivakumar predicting thumping victory for Congress in the 2004 elections. The same 'Guruji' continued to be consulted by Singh too.

Singh had performed rituals at Kukke Subramanya Temple at the behest of Dwarakanath 'Guruji'. Dwarakanath had become so close to the CM that a road in Chamarajpet area of Bangalore came to be named after his father. I was also aware that Singh had implicit faith in Shadakshari Shivayogi Siddarameshwara Swamiji, the pontiff of Jidaga Math in Aland taluk of Gulbarga district. I had seen the Swamiji staying in Singh's house in Bangalore when Singh was the Home Minister. The Swamiji had predicted that Singh would become the Chief Minister and the CM had great faith in him.

I was also aware that SM Krishna, as the Chief Minister, had once invited the seer of Pejawar Math Visweshwara Tirtha Swamiji to his residence 'Anugraha'. When the visit was cancelled at the last minute, the CM was quite disappointed. Consultation with astrologers, Godmen, visits to Mathas etc were second nature to political personages and I was not surprised by the reaction of Singh for the prediction given by an astrologer.

The very next day, I learnt that a delegation of Congressmen comprising DK Shivakumar, RL Jalappa, H Vishwanath, Benki Mahadev, TB Jayachandra, V Muniyappa, and Dr G Parameshwara were meeting the AICC President on January 7. The aim was to press for either a change in the Congress leadership in the State or going for mid-term elections. Singh pre-empted them by meeting Ahmed Patel and AK Antony along with his supporters on January 5 itself.

After this meeting, the CM told me that the high command was inclined to forge alliances with both JD(S) and AIPJD in the Zilla Parishads depending on the local situation. He also stated that the high command was of the opinion that Congress had a great chance of winning the midterm elections if called. Dharam Singh was quite worried over this development. He once again consulted astrologer Dwarkanath.

When I met Singh on January 8, he was in a sombre mood and said, "Everything is over. My days are numbered." Singh was going to Kudala Sangama for a function and as he came out of his house he saw KK Murthy in the portico and told him that he is going to Kudala Sangama. Murthy corrected him and told him that it is inauspicious to say that one is going. He said in Kannada, "*hoguttini annabedi, hogibittu barteeni anta heli*" (Don't say that you are going, say that you are going and returning). The CM replied, "Anyway, I am going. Everything is over now." He appeared very dejected.

I sat with him in his car and on the way to the airport we discussed the current situation and considered three probable scenarios. They were:

(i) The Congress breaking away with the JD(S) resulting in the JD(S) and the BJP forming a government.

(ii) The Congress breaking the JD(S) by wooing one-third of its legislators.

(iii) Imposition of the President's Rule and going for elections in April 2006 along with Kerala and Tamil Nadu.

The CM stated that those leaders in the Congress party, including Mallikarjuna Kharge, who were planning a liaison with Siddaramaiah, did not know that courting him (Siddaramaiah) was like courting Bangarappa. He said that Siddaramaiah would place so many demands to join or support the Congress party that it would become very difficult to meet them which would ultimately result in losses and embarrassment to the party.

He said that as the high command had decided to align with the AIPJD for running the Zilla Panchayats, Deve Gowda would definitely withdraw from the government. When I asked the CM as to why he was hesitant to meet Sonia Gandhi along with Deve Gowda and explain the position, he replied that such an act would give an impression that he was after power. He did not want the party leaders to think that he was hungry for power, he said.

The CM told me that he was contemplating recommending to the Governor the dissolution of the Legislative Assembly as had been done by Ramakrishna Hegde in 1984.

After his return from Kudala Sangama the same evening, the CM left for Delhi. When I spoke to him on the telephone, he stated that he would not meet any leaders of his party, but would meet only the Prime Minister. He continued to be in a depressed mood. When he met the media persons in Delhi he didn't give any reaction to the questions asked by them about the political situation in the State. However, I was surprised when the NDTV flashed a news item from Delhi that President's Rule was imminent in Karnataka.

When I met a senior legislator the next day and broached the subject of midterm elections, he categorically stated that no legislator would like to face the electorate. He said,

> "They have spent considerable amounts of money to get elected in 2004 and they would not be inclined to again spend money on elections. Whatever be the games the senior leaders are playing, there will not be any elections

in the near future and there would be a re-alignment among the existing legislators."

January 11 happened to be a holiday because of Bakrid festival and when I met the CM for my daily briefing, he told me that none of the MLAs is prepared for midterm elections. He added that as the elections were scheduled to be held 40 months later, the JD(S) would form the government aligning with the BJP. He said that Deve Gowda would proclaim in public that the tie up with BJP was a result of the efforts of his sons and that he (Deve Gowda) had nothing to do with it. These words indeed became prophetic.

When asked whether along with the 10 MLAs who were with Siddaramaiah, the Congress could not wean away another 30 MLAs of the JD(S) to its fold, Dharam Singh laughed and said such a big number of MLAs cannot be easily influenced. He stated that even if a herculean effort is made by the Congress to split the JD(S), the total number of MLAs would not exceed 107 which meant seeking the support of Independent MLAs. Hence Dharam Singh felt that the next government would be formed by the alliance of the BJP and the JD(S) parties. I was amazed at the political acumen of our CM.

On the evening of the same day, the BJP Legislature Party met at the residence of Yeddyurappa. After the meeting, the media was informed that the party was inclined to go for a mid-term poll. I didn't believe that the BJP would call for elections. Meanwhile, KK Murthy spoke to me and told me that Deve Gowda would agree for forming a coalition government with the BJP. I went to Singh's house to inform these developments but as he was busy performing some *poojas*, I came back without meeting him.

On January 13, I found the CM to be in a good mood. When I mentioned that I had heard that the BJP and JD(S) are likely to have an understanding and form the government, he brushed it aside and told me that he had spoken to Ahmed Patel who in turn had spoken to Deve Gowda and had obtained an assurance that there would be no problem to Singh's government. The CM told me that the crisis would blow over.

While I was sitting with the CM, KK Murthy came and told him that Kharge was quite upset with the CM over an interview the CM had given to the Kannada daily *Vijaya Karnataka*. In that interview, Singh had said that the victory in Panchayat elections should not be attributed only to the Party President (Kharge) and that any victory in any election should be considered as a plus point to the Chief Minister too. Singh was probably right. He had spent considerable time, energy and effort for the success of party candidates in the elections, and rightfully had to share the glory. But he didn't want to antagonise Kharge. Therefore, he told Murthy that the interviewer hadn't reported his statement correctly.

There was never any doubt that the relationship between the CM and Kharge was very cordial. Their friendship was cemented in 1968. It was a great camaraderie between the two which had given them an image of political twins. In the political circles, they were often referred to as Lava-Kusha or Ram-Laxman. They would attend many functions together and consult each other on important matters. Both the leaders would frequent each other's houses and greet family members during important events like birthdays or marriage anniversaries etc. I remember that once I was responsible for delaying the CM on his joint tour with Kharge in Bidar district for almost an hour. Kharge, though inconvenienced by this intrusion of mine didn't mind the delay.

At times, however, people who were very close to them would get an impression that there was an undercurrent of envy between the two. There might have been some amount of distrust too though it never came out in the open. Of course, when they were ministerial colleagues, there was no lack of bonhomie. However, when Singh pipped Kharge for the Chief Minister's post, a sort of uneasy relation appeared to have developed between the two. At least this was the impression discernible at that time.

Singh, who knew about Kharge's feelings, went out of his way to keep Kharge in good humour. That was probably the reason why he denied the statement attributed to him in the interview given to *Vijaya Karnataka* daily. Many a time Kharge would communicate certain delicate matters to Singh through me. For instance, he had asked me to tell the CM to expand his cabinet. On many occasions, his opinion about several decisions taken by Dharam Singh was communicated to the CM by KK Murthy, who was very close to both of them. The communication channel between them was always open.

I knew both Kharge and Singh from my Gulbarga days as an IPS Probationer. Both had functioned as Home Ministers and I had an opportunity to work with them in close proximity. While Singh used to be very warm towards anyone who met him, Kharge, on the other hand, gave an impression of being aloof and a 'no-nonsense' person. He would not engage with people or officers in long conversations unless he knew them very closely. As Home Minister, I rated Kharge better than Singh. As a minister, Kharge would constantly call for review meetings and always had first-hand knowledge about the working of his Department. Officers did not dare to bluff him and he would tick off such officers in no time. I had seen the passion with which Kharge got completed a modern Police Training Centre in Gulbarga city which was initially envisaged by Dharam Singh. He had functioned efficiently in whichever department he had headed. I thought that he would have made an efficient Chief Minister if luck had favoured him.

Naturally, Kharge would have felt bad when he was not chosen as the Congress Legislature Party leader. As a minister, he was senior to Dharam Singh. He had become a minister in the cabinet of Devaraj Urs in 1978. He definitely got the cabinet portfolio he wanted, but that was like getting a consolation prize in a race. When he was made the Pradesh Congress Committee President, he must have been placated. Singh gave an impression that Kharge's support to Siddaramaiah was mostly to spite the coalition partner Deve Gowda.

Those days among the Congressmen, the only senior minister in whom Singh reposed trust was RV Deshpande.

If one imagines the pressures and pulls that Singh used to be subjected to, one cannot but admire Singh for performing such a tightrope walk. On the one hand, he was virtually under the thumb of JD(S) leaders and had to act as per their wishes even at the risk of antagonising his own party colleagues. On the other hand, many leaders of his party wanted to see him vacate the CM's *gaddi* at the earliest.

Many followers of SM Krishna had been very unhappy about the fate meted out to their leader and were taking pot shots at the CM whenever an opportunity arose. In his own party, Dharam Singh was supported by only a handful of people. Apart from some leaders in Delhi, very few senior Congressmen declared their support to him. And to add to his woes, the BJP which had 79 MLAs would try to embarrass the government whenever an opportunity arose.

Though by the second week of January 2005, the CM was aware that a crisis was at hand, he was confident that it would blow over. The Planning Commission had increased the plan outlay to Karnataka State by a whopping ₹2,600 crores which were beyond anyone's expectation. A member of the Planning Commission had appreciated the CM as 'very progressive' and had commended his stand on Naxalism. Ahluwalia (Dy Chairman) had praised the efforts being made by the government for the development of Bangalore. The praise by the Planning Commission had elevated the mood of the CM.

When I mentioned to SV Ranganath, Secretary to the CM, about the jubilant mood of the CM, he told me that the financial position of the State was very good at that time and with the bounty given by the Planning Commission, there was a lot of scope for developmental activities. He said that over ₹30,000 crore investments were coming to Karnataka and that was the time to act. He asked me to persuade Singh to spend at least one hour every day only for administrative matters. I knew how difficult this task was. The CM was in such a political situation that administration was the last thought on his mind. I knew that the CM was more interested in his survival rather than on governance. Whatever praise the State got from the Planning Commission was due to the efforts of the bureaucracy, more so of Ranganath himself.

'Genius' Officer

Ranganath, an IAS officer of 1975 batch, was ideally suited for the CM's office. He was an outstanding bureaucrat and had a phenomenal memory. He was one of the most hardworking officers in the country. Whatever praise Dharam Singh had received either from the Planning Commission or his own party leaders was mostly due to the sane advice given by Ranganath. Ranganath would often tell me that Chief Ministers should always concentrate on the well-being of the State.

When I met the CM on January 14, he described Ranganath as a 'genius'. During our meeting that day with the CM, he ruled out snap polls in the State because of the reluctance of the MLAs for elections. Analysing the results of the Panchayat elections, he said that JD(S) was the major gainer and when compared to Panchayat elections of 2000, the Congress had lost some ground. He stated that the performance of the AIPJD of Siddaramaiah was not at all impressive as the party had won only about 40 seats while it had contested hundreds. He thought that the visit to Mumbai by DK Shivakumar, V Muniyappa, CM Lingappa, and Gandsi Shivaramu with the aim of getting the support of SM Krishna to destabilise his government would prove futile. He said that there would be realignment between the political parties to form a new government if his government fell and that in all probabilities the BJP and the JD(S) would form the next government. He said that the BJP-JD(S) combine would not be convenient to the Congress party when it was facing elections to the four States shortly. He was, therefore, confident that somehow the Congress and the JD(S) would sort out whatever differences that had cropped up between them and that there would be no problem for his government.

When I naively asked him whether he had made his analysis known to the Congress high command, he smiled and said that he would be sending Dr G Parameshwara and Prof BK Chandrasekhar to meet Sonia Gandhi and Ahmed Patel to explain the situation and save his government. He told me that Prakash Karat was slated to meet Sonia Gandhi soon and explain to her how an alliance with the AIPJD would not be beneficial to the Congress party. He also stated that if the Left parties, the NCP and the JD(S) decided to leave the coalition at the Centre, the UPA government would fall and hence Sonia Gandhi would take Karat seriously.

I had also learnt by then that certain leaders of the Congress party, belonging to the 'Kuruba' community, to which Siddaramaiah belonged to, led by former Minister H Vishwanath, were drumming up support to prevent Siddaramaiah's entry into the Congress. I had been told that a delegation of 'Kuruba' leaders had also met SM Krishna in Mumbai and tried to convince him to prevent the entry of Siddaramaiah into the Congress.

On January 16th, Dharam Singh told me that his party bosses had sent a representative to assess the mood of the Congress legislators and that he was sure that none of them would seek elections. He said that if a need arose, he would himself announce on the floor of the house that if the legislators wanted he would submit his government's resignation. Though he knew that his seat was shaky a glimmer of hope was still glowing in his heart.

The CM later asked me to make a quick assessment about the seats that would be won by each party if the elections were to be held within the next six months to the State Assembly. We made an assessment and told the CM that if elections were to be held immediately, the Congress would get 108 seats; the JD(S)-49 seats; the BJP-46 seats; Independents-12 seats; AIPJD and all others-10 seats.

When I presented my assessment to the CM, I also told him that the BJP legislators were discussing about forming the next government and that the senior leaders of the party, namely, HN Ananth Kumar, BS Yeddyurappa, Jagadish Shettar, and KS Eshwarappa had proceeded to Delhi to consult their party leaders. The next morning, Venkaiah Naidu arrived at Bangalore from Delhi. The JD(S) legislators who held a meeting at Silver Oak resorts at Yelahanka, Bangalore, resolved that Kumaraswamy was their leader and gave a letter to that effect. Dore Raju, the Legal Advisor to the BJP met the JD(S) legislators in the resort. While informing these developments to the CM, I told him that we had Intelligence that Kumaraswamy with forty MLAs would break up from the JD(S) party and would form an alliance with the BJP. At that time the JD(S) had the strength of 58 MLAs.

The CM immediately phoned KK Murthy and shared this information with him. Murthy stated that he would talk to Deve Gowda and let the CM know shortly. Meanwhile, Deve Gowda had told media persons that the coalition government would not be disturbed at any cost.

While I was certain that Kumaraswamy would go along with the BJP, the CM still had 'fond' hopes that the former PM would prevent his son from doing anything drastic. Venkaiah Naidu told the media that his party had not yet spoken to JD(S), keeping the hopes of the CM alive. What surprised me was that the Congress high command which was aware of the fast-moving political developments in the State had maintained a stoic silence.

15

Fast Moving Political Developments

After attending a review meeting on law and order in the CM's office at Vidhana Soudha on the afternoon of January 18, 2006, I told the CM that the end of his government was near. He did not react.

That morning, at the corridors of Vidhana Soudha, I had met Nafeez Fazal, a former minister. She told me that she had telephoned Pillay, personal secretary to Sonia Gandhi a few hours ago to brief him about the political situation in Karnataka. When she told him that the government would not last, Pillay reportedly replied *Jaane Do* (Let it go). She had opined that the Congress high command was not at all worried about the developments in Karnataka.

Around 4 PM the same day, I received information from the ADC to the Governor (who was from the police department) that Kumaraswamy had sought an appointment with the Governor for 6 PM, stating that he would be meeting the Governor along with some MLAs. I went to the CM who was in his residence 'Anugraha' and shared this news. He summoned RV Deshpande and DK Shivakumar and held consultations. Both of them suggested that the CM should dissolve the Legislative Assembly. I was in touch with Raj Bhavan and learnt that 37 MLAs of the JD(S) along with Kumaraswamy had already arrived at Raj Bhavan and were waiting to meet the Governor. I conveyed this news to the CM and the two senior leaders. The first reaction of the CM was that only 37 out of the 40 MLAs had come to Raj Bhavan and they were three short. I didn't fathom the reason for this reaction because 37 JD(S) MLAs with 79 of the BJP were sufficient to form a coalition government. Probably the CM had meant that out of the 40 MLAs who were earlier thought to support Kumaraswamy three had backed out.

The CM decided to call an emergency meeting of the State Cabinet and notices were sent to the ministers post haste. From the JD(S), MP Prakash, PGR Sindhia, and HS Mahadev Prasad were the only ones to attend. The Cabinet expressed its support to Dharam Singh. In the meanwhile, all the BJP legislators met the Governor and gave a letter stating that they would support Kumaraswamy.

Later on, Deve Gowda spoke to the CM and told him that Kumaraswamy had no *locus standi* in the party as he (Gowda) was the National President of the Party and that MP Prakash was the JDLP leader. He stated that he had spoken to the Governor requesting him not to consider the letter of Kumaraswamy about withdrawing support to the government.

This assurance by Deve Gowda brought some hopes to the CM. He decided to meet the Governor and sought an appointment. Meanwhile, Yeddyurappa announced that the Joint Legislature Party of the BJP/JD(S) had unanimously elected Kumaraswamy as its leader. Deve Gowda also gave a press statement that it was the saddest day of his life and that he had nothing to do with his son's actions. Meanwhile, my officers had told me that a *shamiana* had been put up in Deve Gowda's Padmanabha Nagar residence to welcome the legislators on their return from Raj Bhavan.

The same night at 10 PM, the CM met the Governor along with Kharge, HK Patil and PGR Sindhia and sought time to prove his majority on the floor of the House. The legislature session had already been slated to begin the very next day and hence the Governor agreed with this request and fixed January 30 as the day to prove the strength of the government on the floor of the House. Singh was happy about this outcome. But he was thoroughly dejected over the course of the events that day. He put on a brave face. I knew Antony and Ahmed Patel had already spoken to Deve Gowda that night, but Singh felt that the high command had not really applied its mind over the political situation in Karnataka.

High Drama

The next morning, on January 19, Venkaiah Naidu led all the BJP legislators to Raj Bhavan and sat in a protest demanding that the Governor should refrain from addressing the Joint Legislature Session. Their contention was that the speech to be read by the Governor had been prepared by the Congress-JD(S) government which had lost its majority. Governor TN Chaturvedi told them that he would stick to the rule book and went to Vidhana Soudha for delivering his address. In the corridors of Vidhana Soudha, rumours had spread that the Congress had offered the same terms to Kumaraswamy as the BJP and had requested him to continue the coalition between the Congress and the JD(S). Kumaraswamy vehemently denied these rumours. Meanwhile, the Governor told the press that the government had to prove its majority on the floor of the house on January 27. The government had, therefore, been given almost eight days time to prove its majority and this was reasonable.

On January 20, the CM was bombarded with suggestions as to how to save his government and he was thoroughly confused. When he had some time for me, he said in Kannada, *Ella Mugeetu* (Everything is over). He said that his party leaders had failed to see the writing on the wall. He said that the leaders didn't take his prediction of the BJP coming to power in Karnataka very seriously. He wasn't sure whether the State Party President Kharge had briefed the high command about the imminent political scenario in Karnataka moving towards formation of a BJP government.

During the day some leaders of the Congress made efforts to persuade Kumaraswamy to change his mind. S Ramesh who went as an emissary met Kumaraswamy. He later reported that there was no possibility of any rapprochement as Kumaraswamy had told Ramesh that he didn't trust the Congress. Kumaraswamy had feared that if he agreed to any 'counter-offer' by the Congress of making him the CM, the party might withdraw support midway and make him a laughing stock.

HDK for BJP

Kumaraswamy is said to have referred to how the Congress party had pulled the rug under the feet of Deve Gowda when Gowda was the Prime Minister. He also reportedly told Ramesh that he had made a gentleman's promise to the BJP and he would not like to go back on it. After learning about Kumaraswamy's feelings, I suggested to the CM that as there was no possibility of saving his government, it would be better he resigned. He didn't react.

On January 20, *Deccan Herald*, English daily published from Bangalore, wrote that no tear will be shed for Dharam Singh. I tended to agree with that assessment. The same newspaper carried a news item the very next day mentioning that Kumaraswamy had stated that the State Intelligence had failed to take note of the political developments in the State. Both Dharam Singh and I knew how wrong the 'future CM' was if indeed he had been correctly quoted by the newspaper.

Probably on reading the newspaper Kharge telephoned me on the morning of January 21 and asked me whether I had not given any timely inputs about the impending political developments to the CM. I replied that the writing on the wall was for everybody to see. When I mentioned Kharge's call to me and to the CM, he said that it is natural for politicians to wriggle out of the situation by putting the blame on the Intelligence Wing.

The very next day the CM gave an interview to *The Indian Express* newspaper (published on January 22, 2006) that the

State Intelligence had indeed given him inputs about the impending alliance between the BJP and the JD(S). To the specific question, "Were you surprised by the sudden developments?" put by the interviewer G Virat Singh, the CM replied as follows:

> "As a Chief Minister, I had Intelligence reports about the movements, meetings and the conclaves that the political parties had convened. But I did not except such a serious move by a section of the MLAs belonging to a particular party. In my reply to the House when I seek the confidence vote, I will explain in detail what might have gone wrong."

To another question, "How do you react to the charge that you have humiliated JD(S) MLAs and interfered in the transfer of officials connected with JD(S) ministries?," the CM replied:

> "In 34 years of my political career, I have not humiliated anyone. The charge against me is itself a reply to some of my Congress colleagues who accused me of surrendering to the JD(S) at the cost of Congress."

To the next question, "Do you agree with the view held by many, including Siddaramaiah that the toppling is Deve Gowda's ploy to make his son Kumaraswamy the Chief Minister?", Dharam Singh said:

> "No, it is neither a ploy, nor a drama. I can tell you from my long association with Deve Gowda that he has not been dishonest with me so far. He has been trying to persuade his son Kumaraswamy not to ally with the BJP as it is communal."

The CM was very much aware of what was happening around him. Though he knew that the ground under him was slipping away, like a drowning person hoping that a piece of straw would save him, Dharam Singh hoped that somehow Deve Gowda would prevail on Kumaraswamy to continue the alliance.

The Intelligence Wing was only one channel through which any CM would get information about what was happening. A CM would meet hundreds of persons every day and whether he/she likes it or not, would come to know about any major happening and any unfolding event. Seasoned politicians such as Dharam Singh had the immense political maturity to know how the political wind was blowing and didn't need inputs from Intelligence agencies for the same. Probably such leaders depended on Intelligence inputs only to confirm what they knew all along. If an officer of any Intelligence agency believed that he had more political acumen than his masters, he would be living in a fool's paradise.

When I was sitting with the CM that day, DK Shivakumar came to meet him seeking a favour. The CM had by then been told by the Chief Secretary not to pass any orders on any file as it would be struck down by the next government. Important and sensitive files were also not sent to the CM for his orders. After Shivakumar left, the CM remarked that the person who plotted the fall of his government had 'remorselessly' come to him seeking favours. He also told me that his predicament was caused by his party leaders SM Krishna, DK Shivakumar, BL Shankar and others inimical to Deve Gowda. He rued that for the sake of controlling only two Zilla Panchayats, Mysore and Mandya, his government was being sacrificed.

In the 40 members Zilla Panchayat of Mandya, the JD(S) had secured 18 seats, the Congress 16 and the AIPJD 5. In the 46 member Mysore ZP, the Congress had secured 18 seats, the JD(S) 11, the AIPJD 16 seats and the result of one seat was yet to be announced. Former Ministers H Vishwanath in Mysore and MH Ambareesh in Mandya had vehemently opposed any alliance with the JD(S) to control the ZPs. Vishwanath had dared Deve Gowda to withdraw support to the government. He reportedly said, "I challenge Gowda and the working President of Janata Dal (Secular) HD Kumaraswamy to withdraw from the coalition if they have the guts to do so" when presspersons reminded him of the JD(S) leaders' recent threat in that regard. Ambareesh had threatened *en masse* resignation from the party.

The CM stated for the current political problems, his party men from Tumkur, Kolar, Mysore and Mandya districts were to be blamed. When I suggested to him to make his feelings public in the forthcoming AICC session at Hyderabad, he said that it would not make any difference. He said when his party didn't pull up the KPCC President for appointing BL Shankar to negotiate with Siddaramaiah, whatever he would say in the AICC session would fall on deaf ears.

Dharam Singh was very close with Yeddyurappa and I am certain that the BJP leader would have given enough indications of what was happening to him. Though Yeddyurappa was not seen around Singh very much during late December 2005 and early January 2006, I was sure that their channel of communication was open. My own feeling was that Singh depended too much on the assurances given by Deve Gowda and acceding to all and sundry requests of JD(S) leaders which were his undoing. I also felt that he didn't concentrate on administration and didn't take control of many situations.

A lot of political developments happened between January 22 and 27. The CM attended the AICC session at Hyderabad on January 23. When I spoke to him on phone, he told me that Sonia Gandhi had summoned DK Shivakumar and RL Jalappa the previous evening and had reprimanded them. He said that a majority of AICC members wanted the coalition between the Congress and the JD(S) to continue and that the high command would do its best to keep the BJP away from coming to power in Karnataka. He stated that the Party President had called a meeting of Mallikarjuna Kharge, AK Antony and himself and had told them that she would try to get the problem sorted out. She was slated to meet Deve Gowda the next day.

I had learnt from my sources that Gowda would put forth five demands before the AICC President. Those were –

(a) The Congress party should not associate with Siddaramaiah and AIPJD.
(b) Action to be taken against SM Krishna, RL Jalappa, DK Shivakumar, BL Shankar and VS Ugrappa.
(c) Removal of Kharge from the post of KPCC President.
(d) To follow the Maharashtra pattern of coalition in toto.
(e) Constitution of a coordination committee for day-to-day administration.

I was told that if these conditions were agreed by the Congress President, the coalition government would survive.

A senior journalist from a leading newspaper had told me that YSV Datta, a close confidante of Gowda, had told her that whatever was the public posture of Deve Gowda, he would not like to have an understanding with the BJP. I telephonically informed the same to CM at Hyderabad. The same night the CM returned to Bangalore.

Rituals

On January 24, while Gowda went to Delhi to meet AK Antony and Pranab Mukherjee before calling on Sonia Gandhi, Dharam Singh immersed himself in performing various *poojas* and rituals. I learnt that the meetings with Congress leaders went off well and the leaders had taken the time to respond to the request of Gowda.

On the next day, the CM continued various rituals at his residence. He appeared to be morose and told me that the chances of survival of his government were 50:50. Kumaraswamy gave a statement later in the day that he would not go with the Congress. Both Deve Gowda and KK Murthy told the CM that they were hopeful that Kumaraswamy would change his mind. On the morning of 26, I attended the Republic Day Parade and later on joined the CM for breakfast. He asked me whether everything was over. As I was not used to giving diplomatic replies, I replied in the affirmative.

A few hours later AK Antony landed in Bangalore. Gowda left for Sringeri with his wife. Antony held a brief meeting with both the CM and Mallikarjuna Kharge. After his return from Sringeri, Gowda went to the residence of Venkatesh, proprietor of *Eesanje* evening newspaper. Soon after that, all the 37 MLAs owing allegiance to Kumaraswamy trooped into Venkatesh's house. I was told that Gowda held a meeting there and asked the MLAs to reconsider their decision and the MLAs had refused his request.

On the morning of January 27, my colleague in the IPS, Narayana Gowda spoke to me and informed that there was one more meeting between Gowda and the 37 MLAs. However, there was no change in the stand of the MLAs. I knew that he was quite close to the family of the former Prime Minister even before he joined the IPS and hence believed him.

The MLAs of JD(S) were adamant to forge an alliance with the BJP. They all came together to attend the legislature session.

As the session began, Vatal Nagaraj objected to the presence of two officials from Raj Bhavan sitting in the officers' gallery. This delayed the proceedings. The obituary references and other matters went on till 3 PM. Later the Speaker Krishna announced that he recognised Kumaraswamy as the Leader of the Janata Dal Legislature Party. This resulted in commotion. The speaker had been elected as an MLA from KR Pet constituency of Mandya district on JD(S) ticket. Many Congress MLAs rushed to the well of the house and began shouting. They stated that they had no confidence in the Speaker himself. The Speaker adjourned the house twice. When the House reassembled, the CM moved a motion of no confidence against the Speaker. He, however, did not table the motion of confidence citing that the House was not in order. The Speaker adjourned the house *sine die* and announced that he would report the matter to the Governor. I witnessed the entire house proceedings that day which was more exciting than watching a thriller movie.

While so much activity was taking place inside the House, a number of in-camera meetings were being held by AK Antony and Venkaiah Naidu outside the House with several groups of legislators.

Deve Gowda meanwhile announced that he was resigning from his post of the National President of the JD(S) and wrote a letter to AK Antony requesting him to ask the CM to submit his resignation. This riled Antony and he was fuming with anger. At 8 PM, the CM went to Raj Bhavan along with Antony and met the Governor. The Governor reportedly told them that he would give a decision the next day.

Dharam Singh Resigns

On the morning of January 28 when I met the CM, he was in a depressed mood. He justified his action in seeking a no-confidence against the Speaker. He told me that he informed the Governor that while he was not hesitant to face the vote of confidence, the action of the Speaker in recognising Kumaraswamy as Leader of the JDLP post-haste was objectionable. The ball, he said, was in the Governor's court.

The Governor too seemed to have a limited choice. As Singh had not tabled the motion of confidence, he could give a chance to the CM by asking the Speaker to convene a short session of the Legislature or he could straightway dismiss the government. Around 11 AM, the CM went to Raj Bhavan and met the Governor. After he returned, he asked SV Ranganath to draft the letter of resignation. After Singh signed the resignation letter, Ranganath personally delivered it to Raj Bhavan.

Dharam Singh held a press conference soon after and announced his resignation. He was, however, criticised by the Media and several other political observers that his resignation had come a day too late. I also had felt that had he announced stepping down on the floor of the house, it would have been more graceful. His resignation had come exactly twenty months after assumption of office.

During this press conference Singh recited the lines from an Urdu poem, which were as follows: "*Na jaane kin kin ki dua me rahte hai hum, dushman dubana chahata hai, lekin samandar uchal deta hai.*" (One doesn't know under whose blessings one remains/the enemy wants to drown me but the sea throws me back on the shore.)

The Governor accepted Dharam Singh's resignation and invited Kumaraswamy to form the government. On coming to know that Kumaraswamy had gone to the Raj Bhavan, I rushed there and met him. The Chief Secretary was also present there. I congratulated both Kumaraswamy and Yeddyurappa and sought details about the swearing-in ceremony. The CM designate told me that it would be held on the grand steps of Vidhana Soudha on February 3 at 3 PM.

For the first time, I saw Yeddyurappa not knitting his eyebrows but beaming with happiness.

At Raj Bhavan, I took N Cheluvaraya Swamy, MLA and close confidante of Kumaraswamy, aside and told him that I would be completing almost three years as Head of State Intelligence and would like to make way for the new chief of Intelligence. He told me that Kumaraswamy had confidence in me and that he would speak to the CM designate about my request. I had made a similar request to Dharam Singh when he had taken over as the CM. As Kumaraswamy had recently commented adversely about the State Intelligence Wing which I headed, I didn't want to continue under the new dispensation.

On the morning of January 29, I met Dharam Singh who was continuing as the interim CM and told him about the swearing-in of the new government. Singh told me the details of what had transpired in the previous days. He said that when Antony arrived in Bangalore, Deve Gowda had gone off to Sringeri and with great difficulty when Singh contacted Gowda and asked him to meet Antony, Gowda had replied that he would call at 5 PM, on his return to Bangalore and fix the time and venue of the meeting.

When Gowda didn't call the CM at 5 PM, Singh contacted him again and was told that the meeting could be fixed in the night. Accordingly, a room was booked in Hotel Windsor Manor where Antony went at 8 PM and waited for Gowda's arrival. Antony was made to wait for three hours. Finally, at 11 PM, Deve Gowda went there. Antony supposedly told Gowda that his party had accepted all the five demands put forth by Gowda before Sonia Gandhi a few days ago. Gowda told him that he would convince his son Kumaraswamy and get back the next day.

Around 1 AM (in the night), Antony came to the CM's residence. At 1.30 AM, the CM received a call from Sonia Gandhi asking him whether everything was all right. The CM had replied that he hoped for the best. At about 8 AM on January 27, Gowda spoke to the CM and asked him to resign and come to Raj Bhavan and that he too would come to Raj Bhavan along with Kumaraswamy and all the MLAs and a solution would be found. Singh was flabbergasted by this request and rushed to Antony. Antony advised the CM not to resign as it was a ploy by JD(S) and to seek the vote of confidence.

Within a few minutes, Deve Gowda sent words to Antony that he wanted three more hours to give a final answer and hence the drama in the assembly. At the end of three hours, Gowda sent a letter to Antony through YSV Datta that Dharam Singh should resign as he (Gowda) had failed to convince his son Kumaraswamy. The letter infuriated Antony because of which Singh didn't seek the vote of confidence.

I informed the CM that the Speaker had sent a scathing report against him to the Governor and the Governor was very upset with the CM. Singh said,

> "After I came back from Raj Bhavan on the afternoon of January 28, I called Madam. She was in a meeting with the PM. She took the call and told me that I had done well but now I should resign. I, therefore, sent my resignation letter immediately to the Governor."

Dharam Singh told me that he had spoken to the Prime Minister that day and that the PM was very sympathetic to him and told him that none from Karnataka would be included in the Central cabinet which was being expanded that very day.

He also said that DK Shivakumar was aiming to become the Leader of the Opposition and that he (Singh) was not aspiring for any position.

On the same evening, the Union Cabinet was expanded. Dharam Singh was happy that while Shinde, Governor of Andhra Pradesh, was included in the cabinet, neither SM Krishna, the Governor of Maharashtra, nor any other politician from Karnataka was included.

Meanwhile, both HD Kumaraswamy and BS Yeddyurappa went temple hopping. Compared to his two predecessors, Kumaraswamy was more inclined towards visits to temples, belief in Vaastu, astrology and the like.

Vatal Nagaraj, and MLAs S Rajendran and GV Sreerama Reddy filed a petition in the High Court seeking disqualification of Kumaraswamy. Political observers felt that Nagaraj might be acting at the behest of Dharam Singh or his supporters. It was Nagaraj who had created a ruckus in the house during the vote of confidence session and had delayed the proceedings. I do not know whether Nagaraj was acting as per someone's cue. As Deve Gowda had sought three hours' time from Antony to give a reply to the proposal by the Congress, the proceedings had to be somehow delayed.

Political observers had felt that both Deve Gowda and Kumaraswamy were acting in tandem and that it was a drama played by the father-son duo to topple the Dharam Singh government. In its issue dated 22nd January 2006, *The Economic Times* had written,

> "Even when the family drama is being played out on the Karnataka stage, there are those working overtime to pre-empt the scripted denouement! Chief among them is Siddaramaiah whom Deve Gowda expelled from the party

some months ago for projecting himself as the leader of the Backward Classes while serving as JD(S) LP leader and Deputy Chief Minister in the Dharam Singh government. In fact, it was the perceived proximity of Siddaramaiah to a section of the Karnataka Congress that caused the most recent rift in the present coalition government."

16

New Government Takes Office

It had been decided that both the coalition partners, the JD(S) and the BJP would share power on a 20-20 basis. During the first 20 months, Kumaraswamy would be the CM and in the next 20 months, Yeddyurappa would hold the reins of the State. Initially, only two persons, HD Kumaraswamy as the CM and BS Yeddyurappa as the Deputy CM would be sworn-in and the cabinet would be expanded later. The vote of confidence would be sought on February 8.

On February 1 and 2, I attended a series of meetings convened to plan the swearing-in ceremony of the new government. Cheluvaraya Swamy attended one such meeting and spelt out what the CM-designate wanted. On the morning of February 3, I attended the swearing-in ceremony of the new government which took place on the grand steps of Vidhana Soudha. The occasion was historic in more than one sense. It was for the first time in Karnataka a father and son had occupied the post of the CM.

Only two persons, Kumaraswamy and Yeddyurappa took oaths as CM and Deputy CM respectively. Deve Gowda was conspicuous by his absence. The gesture of Dharam Singh in attending the ceremony was appreciated by everyone present. Kumaraswamy later told the media that before coming to the oath-taking ceremony he went to the residence of Singh to seek his blessings and Singh didn't show an iota of rancour towards Kumaraswamy who was the root cause of Singh's loss of power.

During the ceremony, my colleague in the IPS, Narayana Gowda who was seen closely moving with the 'first' family took me aside and told me that while I would be transferred out of the Intelligence Department, I would be given a 'good' posting. He told me that everyone in Deve Gowda's family, except HD Revanna, had a very good opinion of me. He asked me that whatever post I desired would be given to me by Kumaraswamy.

I had regularly interacted with the new CM for almost twenty months. Before contesting Assembly elections in 2004, he had been elected as a Member of Lok Sabha from the Kanakapura constituency. He had sought re-election in 1998 and had lost. I had found him to be very amiable and genial person. He had a lot of patience and perseverance. He didn't bulldoze his way to get things done but believed in persuasion. He was found more in the company of friends than his family members. He was reverential towards his father and elder brothers. One of his elder brothers Balakrishna Gowda had earlier worked in Karnataka Government and had taken voluntary retirement before Kumaraswamy became the CM.

God Fearing HDK

Kumaraswamy had tremendous political acumen which he had amply demonstrated by toppling the Congress-JD(S) coalition government. He had a very sharp mind and would assimilate the briefings from officers quite fast. While his immediate two predecessors were fond of tennis and Urdu poetry, he was very much interested in Kannada film industry as he was an exhibitor, distributor, and producer of movies himself. He had produced five movies. Hence he would be quite at ease with film personalities. It was rumoured that he had also married a Kannada film actress.

A prominent trait I had found in him was his abiding interest in visiting temples and godmen, like many others in his family. He had his share of controversies but had not allowed them to hinder his progress in politics.

On the morning of February 4, I tried to meet the CM for my daily briefing about the developments in the State but could not meet him. I learnt that he had left for Nonavinakere in Tumkur district by a helicopter. I was told he was visiting a Swamiji who was known for his astrological prowess. When I met the CM after his return, he asked me to brief me about the Police Department in Karnataka, its strengths and its weaknesses. I gave him a very objective picture of the police department highlighting its weak points too.

About two hours later, the CM addressed all the top level police officers in Karnataka and told them what his priorities were. He extensively used the inputs given by me a few hours ago. The officers appeared baffled by his knowledge about the department's working. Thankfully they didn't know that I was the one who had scripted his talk. During the meeting, the CM gave an impression as a man in a hurry. He had clearly set goals and priorities for the police department.

When I went to the chambers of the Deputy CM, I could not but help recall my first meeting with BS Yeddyurappa. It was in the latter part of 1991. As the Deputy Inspector General of Police of North Eastern Range, Gulbarga, I had been to Munirabad in the then Raichur district for official work. I was staying in the iconic Kailas Guest House by the side of Tungabhadra dam. As I was leaving the Guest House, Yeddyurappa arrived there. He got down from his car, greeted me with folded hands and introduced himself. I had told him that he was quite well-known and there was no need for him to introduce himself and I too belonged to Karnataka State. I knew that he had been elected to the Legislative Assembly for the second time from Shikaripura in Shimoga district.

The next time I met him was in 1996 when I was working as Police Commissioner Hubli-Dharwad.

On August 22, 1996, Deve Gowda, as Prime Minister of India, had come to Hubli to inaugurate a renovated Railway workshop. The citizens of Hubli in general and the BJP workers, in particular, were extremely unhappy with Gowda over his move to shift the Headquarters of the proposed South

Western Railway Zone from Hubli to Bangalore. What they couldn't fathom was that it was Deve Gowda who was instrumental in getting the Zone for Hubli.

The BJP members had planned massive protests and demonstrations during the PM's visit. As the Police Commissioner of Hubli-Dharwad then, it was my duty to see that the visit went off without a hitch. As the Central Intelligence agencies had given a report that there would be ugly incidents during the visit, the Special Protection Group tasked with the PM's security didn't want to take any chances. The State DG and IGP had also been told to beef up security.

A few days before the visit, Madiyal, Additional DGP in-charge of Law and Order then, was sent to Hubli to oversee the security arrangements. Madiyal had worked in the Special Protection Group for more than five years. When he came to Hubli he went through the bandobust plan that I had drafted and was satisfied. He told me that as the Police Commissioner of the twin cities, the primary responsibility for the PM's security was mine and mine alone and that he would only help me do my work and not interfere in my arrangements. Very few officers would take such a stand. Most senior police officers would have tried to take over the security arrangements from the Commissioner and claim a credit if everything went well and blame the subordinate officers if anything went wrong. But Madiyal was made of a different calibre.

The SPG sent a big team for advance security liaison to work with me. When the PM landed in Hubli in his special aircraft, over 30 SPG men did ring round security for him. To oversee their work, an officer of the rank of IGP had been drafted. In normal circumstances an SP rank officer would accompany the PM. IGP Joshi of the SPG who accompanied the PM was my course mate when I attended a training course in England in 1991.

Along with Prime Minister Deve Gowda, Ratnakar Rao, Secretary (Security), Ministry of Home Affairs, Government of India, Shyamal Datta, Joint Director in-charge of VIP Security in the Intelligence Bureau, New Delhi and SA

Subbaiah, Additional DGP, State Intelligence, Bangalore, came to Hubli. This was unprecedented indeed.

The PM was taken in an unusually big convoy to the venues of his functions. I had made elaborate arrangements to see that no protestor came anywhere near the Prime Minister or his convoy. A group of persons tried to wave black flags, but they were taken into custody much before the PM's convoy passed that way. The entire visit passed off without any untoward incident and I was profusely complimented by all the visiting senior officers from Delhi and Bangalore.

BSY's Growth

However, immediately after Deve Gowda's special aircraft took off from the Hubli airport, the BJP workers started a riot. They indulged in large-scale arson and stone pelting resulting in loss of public property. More than half a dozen KSRTC buses were set on fire. We used lathi charge and tear gas to disperse the rioting mobs. And, when the situation didn't come under control, ordered the arrest of all the BJP stalwarts of Hubli which included Vijay Sankeshwar, Member of Parliament, MLAs Jagadish Shettar and Ashok Katwe, Prahlad Joshi, several corporators and party office-bearers. The situation returned to normalcy within a few hours.

I transferred over one hundred arrested leaders to the Police Parade Ground in Dharwad and kept them under preventive custody. Such an action was also unprecedented in Hubli. Top BJP leaders demanded my immediate transfer from Hubli. At that time Yeddyurappa had enquired with me angrily as to why I had taken such an unprecedented action and I had replied that I had no alternative.

During his earlier and subsequent visits to Hubli he had met me twice or thrice and they were related to taking up his party men's requests with me.

I have mentioned about Yeddyurappa's personal request to me when I was ADG, Intelligence with Dharam Singh, to get the Agriculture College Guest House, Dharwad declared as a jail to house Uma Bharti. Thanks to the Chief Minister, his request had been acceded to. In a matter of 25 years, Yeddyurappa had grown in strength too and had almost single-handedly made the BJP a party to reckon with.

Thinking of Yeddyurappa, my thoughts drifted towards another leader Mallikarjuna Kharge. I recalled the many similarities between both these leaders. Both always wore white clothes, one a safari suit and the other dhoti and kurta. Both have serious visages. Both would make unannounced visitors uncomfortable while meeting them. Both had a large fan following. Both had become presidents of their respective political parties at the State level. Both leaders had a political twin in the same party - Dharam Singh with Mallikarjuna Kharge and KS Eshwarappa with Yeddyurappa. Despite their similarities, both Kharge and Yeddyurappa appeared to repel each other like similar magnetic poles.

On February 5th, the Vice President of India arrived in Bangalore and thereafter proceeded to Shravanabelagola. After seeing him at the airport I went to meet the CM at his office. He told me that henceforth he would like to get a briefing from me in his home office 'Krishna' around 9:30 in the morning, as he continued to live in his private house in the southern part of the city.

The next morning when I went to meet the CM Kumaraswamy, he had been closeted with my colleague Shankar Bidari. Bidari had earlier worked as Addl DGP Intelligence when JH Patel was leading the JD(S) government as CM consequent to the elevation of Deve Gowda to the post of PM. I presumed that Bidari must be either trying for my post or he must have been summoned by the CM for some consultations. However, Bidari coming close to the Deve Gowda family had surprised me. I remembered that when he was being posted as IGP, Central Range, Bangalore by Dharam Singh, there was quite a resistance from the JD(S).

After his meeting with the CM, Bidari is said to have informed some of his friends that he discussed politics with the CM.

When I met the CM, I briefed him about the continuing protests by the Scheduled Castes and the competition among the BJP legislators over the allocation of ministerial berths. I also informed him that the Naxals were planning to observe the first death anniversary of Saket Rajan and Shivalingu in a befitting manner and this might pose a problem to the police.

Next day, CM held a high-level meeting regarding the protests by Scheduled Castes. Later the Chief Secretary held a meeting in his office regarding the move by the Naxals to observe the death ceremony of their leader.

On February 8, I had a frank discussion with Kumaraswamy about my transfer from the Intelligence Wing. The job of Addl DGP, Intelligence was quite stressful and I had worked in the same post for almost three years. I was one of the very few officers who had worked as Head of Intelligence for three years, and with three Chief Ministers. Though the new CM was very cordial towards me, I had decided to seek a change. With the DG and IGP repeatedly finding faults with me I had thought a change in posting would do me good.

When the question of my further posting cropped up, the CM said that he was in a dilemma regarding posting me to the coveted post of Police Commissioner of Bangalore city. He stated that when there was already a protest by Scheduled Castes in the State, posting a non-SC/ST officer like me as Commissioner of Police (CP), would create problems.

His reasoning was simple. The incumbent CP and his predecessor were both SC/ST officers. Among the Addl DGP level officers who were in the zone of consideration for the post of CP the seniormost was a woman officer. The second in line was a SC/ST officer. While the third was a north Indian officer, I was the fourth in line. The CM didn't want to consider any of the first three officers. I reminded him that it was he, who 20 months earlier, had asked me to become the Police Commissioner of Bangalore and it was he who had reiterated the same on January 1, the current year. I told him to take a suitable decision and transfer me out of Intelligence Wing. I told him that I was not hankering for any particular post and would be content with any post that he thought would be suitable for me. He replied that he would think about it and closed the topic.

On the same day, the CM won the vote of confidence on the floor of the Legislative Assembly. The CM was very happy about the votes in support of his government, but the very next day he appeared worried because of some murmurs within the JD(S) Legislature Party. I guessed that like the BJP legislators, the JD(S) legislators might also be pressurising the CM for plum posts in the cabinet.

The problem with the BJP was different. Many of its senior leaders were members of the Legislative Council and they wanted to become ministers. This was not liked by the members of the Legislative Assembly.

On the afternoon of February 11, I accompanied the CM on his tour of Tamil Nadu and Puducherry by helicopter. He visited the Shani temple at Karaikal and at Puducherry he inaugurated a residential complex built by the JSS Matha of Mysore for the victims of Tsunami. By the time he completed all the programmes, it had become dark and the helicopter could not fly back to Bangalore. The CM hence decided to take a flight from Chennai back to Bangalore and we all left Puducherry by road and reached Chennai airport.

At the airport, the CM purchased air tickets for all five of us who had accompanied him in the helicopter from his personal money. This really surprised me.

The next day, the CM went to Hirekerur by helicopter and when I went to see him off at Jakkur airfield, I saw Shankar Bidari and another IPS officer ST Ramesh. I was informed that they had accompanied the CM from his residence in JP Nagar. IPS officers other than the DG and IGP, Commissioner of Police, Bangalore and the Chief of Intelligence would not generally accompany the CM in his car and hence I was surprised. And when Bidari hopped into the CM's helicopter and went to Hirekerur, the surprise became a wonder. Those who were present in the airfield started speculating that Bidari would be the next Addl DGP Intelligence.

As I was on leave for two days, I could meet the CM only on January 15 when he returned from his Delhi tour. I was informed by a journalist friend that while at Delhi, the CM met media persons and during the interaction one journalist asked the CM as to why I continued to work as the Head of Intelligence Wing. I presumed that the journalist must have been prompted by some of my colleagues interested in replacing me. Kumaraswamy is said to have replied that though he had no problems working with me, it was I who had repeatedly requested for a change stating that I was tired of working for three years in the Intelligence Wing and that he would take a suitable decision soon.

The same evening I met Bidari and he indicated to me that he would be succeeding me. He suggested that I should move to his post of Addl DGP Administration. I also met the DG and IGP, Sial that day. He asked me whether he would be continuing in his post. I found his question to be amusing.

Kumaraswamy had asked me to meet him later in the evening. When I met him he told me that the Cabinet would be expanded the very next day and as per the arrangement with the BJP, 7 legislators from the JD(S) and 11 from the BJP would be inducted into the cabinet. He gave me the list of legislators who would be inducted into his ministry and asked me to contact them and inform them to be ready for the swearing-in ceremony. By the time I could communicate this news to the 18 legislators it was already midnight.

The next morning I attended the swearing-in ceremony. In the evening I met my batch-mate ST Ramesh who hinted that the DG and IGP Sial had a dislike towards me and that I would most likely to get a 'lukewarm' appraisal report from him. As the aversion of the DG and IGP towards me was well-known, I was not surprised by this information.

Shifted from Intelligence

On February 20, when I went to meet the CM at his home office, I found my junior colleague Kishore Chandra present there. When I asked him the reason for his presence, he told me that he had been summoned by the CM. Kishore Chandra was at that time working as the Additional Commissioner of Police Bangalore in the rank of Inspector General of Police. He also informed me that he would be replacing me as the Head of the Intelligence Wing. When I told him that the post was that of Addl DGP rank, he stated that the post would be downgraded to the IGP level. For almost a decade an officer of the rank of Addl DGP had headed the Intelligence Wing and downgrading the post of Head of Intelligence would mean finding a new post for an Addl DGP. I thought the move would create cadre management problems.

I also thought that as there were too many IPS officers in the State and also in the Central Intelligence agencies senior in rank to Kishore Chandra, it would be difficult for him to function smoothly. But it was the decision of Kumaraswamy and he had used his prerogative. However, some detractors of the CM commented that after a long time Karnataka had a Chief of Intelligence belonging to the same community as the CM.

Kumaraswamy met both Kishore Chandra and I together in his room and asked us about the burning of a mosque in the outskirts of Bangalore the previous night. We both were clueless and told the CM that we would cause enquiries and report to him later. Kishore Chandra managed to find out that it was a thatched hut which was gutted and not a mosque. That was the reason why the incident had not come to our notice. The CM must have come to know of it through a party worker, we thought.

SV Ranganath, who had continued as the Principal Secretary to the CM, telephoned me in the evening stating that the CM had signed transfer and posting orders of several IPS officers. Kishore Chandra was posted as IGP Intelligence, keeping the post of Addl DGP in abeyance and I was posted as Chairman and Managing Director, Karnataka Police Housing Corporation in place of Srikumar.

Dr Ajay Kumar Singh, Commissioner of Police Bangalore who was expecting his promotion to the rank of Director General of Police was not touched. There would be a lot of freedom in my new post, I thought.

On the morning of February 21, I met the CM in a guest house at Sadashiva Nagar. The CM was using many such places for meeting his colleagues, party men, friends, and others. I used to call them 'safe houses'. (All Intelligence agencies all over the world maintain safe houses for various purposes, especially to protect VIPs from possible terrorist threats). I briefed the CM about the emerging communal tensions in Dakshina Kannada district and the threat to the renowned painter MF Husain by VHP leader Pramod Mutalik, former Bajrang Dal member and the chief of Sri Ram Sene. The CM said that he would talk to his coalition partners about it.

Later the CM raised the topic of my transfer and told me that my posting to Police Housing Corporation was a temporary arrangement and after three months, he would give me whatever posting I desired. I reminded him that he had told me repeatedly that he would post me as Commissioner of Police, Bangalore. Kumaraswamy replied that he had requested Dr Ajai Kumar Singh, Bangalore Police Commissioner, to continue in his post for a further period of three months and that he would consider my case when the Commissioner's post became vacant.

Though the CM was very cordial and gave me an impression of feeling guilty about not keeping his promise, I instinctively knew that I would not be made the Police Commissioner even when Dr Ajai Kumar Singh was promoted. I realised on that day that Kumaraswamy would not honour his promise and would not post me as Commissioner of Police, Bangalore.

I, however, thanked the CM for all the courtesies shown to me and told him that I would hand over charge the moment I received the government order. My transfer order was issued at 1.30 PM that day. At that time I was attending a meeting in the office of the DG and IGP. On coming to know about my transfer, Bidari, who also attended the meeting with me, told me that though Kumaraswamy was a very nice person, he wasn't able to take independent decisions. Bidari said that the CM was bound by pressures exerted by Deve Gowda and Revanna. He said that because of such external pressures the government would come into trouble soon. I remembered what my other colleague Narayana Gowda had told me some weeks ago about HD Revanna's dislike towards me and felt that it might have been a factor about my new posting. I was also quite surprised to note that most senior IPS officers were very unhappy with the IPS postings made by the new government.

The next morning I handed over the post of Chief of Intelligence Wing to Kishore Chandra and assumed charge as Chairman and MD, Karnataka Police Housing Corporation.

17

Beyond Intelligence Work

I had completed 34 months and 12 days as the Chief of Karnataka State Intelligence and was among a handful of officers who have had such a long tenure. I had closely worked with three Chief Ministers consecutively and had seen history in the making from the sidelines.

Working as Additional DGP in the Intelligence Wing had given me lot of exposure to many things. I was lucky to attend the annual conference of Directors General of Police organised by the Intelligence Bureau in Delhi for four consecutive years. I was able to meet top police officers from across the country and learn from their experience. I was able to hear Prime Ministers and Home Ministers give their views of working of the police forces.

I was very lucky to attend the Chief Ministers Conference on Internal Security held in Delhi on April 15, 2005. This was attended by Prime Minister Dr Manmohan Singh. I heard the views of several Chief Ministers on various security concerns facing the country with rapt attention. I was very much impressed by the speech made by the Tamil Nadu CM J Jayalalithaa. I also attended the National Development Council meeting held for two days on June 27 and 28, 2005 which was attended by almost all the Chief Ministers of the country, apart from a galaxy of distinguished persons. I was particularly lucky to attend the 13th National Integration Council meeting in Delhi in September 2005 and listen to top leaders of the country from across the political spectrum. Such an experience rarely comes to a police officer and I consider myself especially lucky.

As Head of the State Intelligence I had the good fortune of knowing the political developments in the State and the country through a variety of media personnel. As I had worked in the State Information Department as its Head earlier I had personally known several journalists from cub reporters to editors. I would regularly meet them and discuss with them the important issues facing the State and pick their brains. As many of them were regularly interacting with top political leaders, I would get to know how the opposition leaders were thinking about any given issue.

One of the journalists whom I used to meet regularly was P Ramaiah. He was formerly working in *The Hindu* and he had retired. Every morning I would meet him during my walks and we would discuss various matters. He had a very fine political sense and made me understand many political nuances. He was later nominated to be a Member of the Legislative Council when the JD(S) government came to power.

I knew VN Subba Rao, former Resident Editor of *The Indian Express* quite closely and would meet him at least once a fortnight. Ishwar Daitota, the Editor of *Vijaya Karnataka* was my personal friend. I would talk to Sachidananda Murthy of *The Week*, and Girish Nikam, formerly of *The Indian Express* in Delhi, whenever I wanted some inputs about what was happening in the corridors of power in the national capital.

Apart from them, I used to be in regular touch with Asha Krishnaswamy, HR Ranganath, Kudli Gururaja, MK Madhusudan, and others.

It is not disputed that many Intelligence outfits depend on the reports that are published in the media. In fact media is known as an 'open source' for Intelligence gathering. When I was working in the Intelligence, visual media had not become as pervasive as it has become now. Nowadays every person who is glued to a television set has access to 'breaking news' 24×7. This has made the work of an Intelligence official difficult. In the earlier years, we would report on law and order matters based on the situation reports sent by our field officers and SPs of districts. Nowadays, even before a district official could sit and draft his report, the top brasses in the State headquarters would have become aware of it.

Redundant Inputs

When I headed the State Intelligence, if I told the CM that a particular political group had met in a resort outside the city, the report would have some 'news value'. Nowadays, the whole world would be aware of such an event and reporting such an event would be considered foolish. The Intelligence officers now need to concentrate more on 'analysing' the events rather than 'reporting' the events. This has become a challenging task indeed.

The challenges we faced were publication/telecast of half baked, ill informed reports. The Chief Minister or senior officials after reading such reports would question me why we had not earlier informed them about the subject in question. It would become difficult for me to convince the powers that be that such reports were without any basis. Fortunately for me 'social media' was almost absent those days and there was no circulation of 'fake news'.

Another challenge that I faced was the bashing by the media or the politicians for what they called 'Intelligence Failure'. Only those persons who have worked in Intelligence agencies know that Intelligence cannot be perfect and failproof. Even if one hundred serious incidents are prevented by timely Intelligence inputs, the media or the public would never come to know of it. But one failure, the Intelligence officer is hung from the first available lamp post. I have already detailed about the terrorist attack in the campus of IISc and have conceded that it was a failure on our part. I have also mentioned many incidents which have been correctly predicted by us. While Intelligence officials are easily castigated for their 'failures', none praises them for their 'successes'. As the proverb goes, "Success has many fathers, but failure is an orphan."

I knew that despite so much criticism levelled against us by the media and the politicians, we had done some good work. Many people were not aware the constraints with which the Intelligence Wing worked. We had a serious shortage of staff. At the time of my handing over charge, there were vacancies of 199 constables, 211 Head Constables, 102 Sub-Inspectors, 43 Inspectors and 2 Deputy Superintendents of Police. Many officers and men posted to Intelligence would try and get transferred out within a few months of their posting to seek 'greener pastures'. As the work in Intelligence Wing was highly specialised, continued attrition of the lower level staff, the workhorse of the Wing, had seriously affected our work.

Recognising this as the most important problem faced by Intelligence Wing, I had submitted a proposal to the government to have direct recruitment of Police Sub-Inspectors and Inspectors. The Intelligence Bureau at the Central Government had such a system. The CID, in our own State, had successfully recruited officers directly from the market. Unfortunately till I handed over the post, no approval had come for such recruitment from the government. When I was the Additional DGP (Recruitment and Training) I succeeded in getting the government order issued. But unfortunately, till this day, no direct recruitment has been made to the State Intelligence.

Right Info

As I handed over charge, I was aware that we had given excellent Intelligence inputs to the district and city police. In March 2004, our operatives had noticed the movement of two top Naxal leaders in Chikmagalur town and helped the local police nab them. In December 2004, we had pointed out to the SP of the same district that a KSRTC bus was likely to be burnt.

On December 24, a bus indeed was set on fire near Sringeri. The police encounter which resulted in killing of Saket Rajan on February 6 was as a result of our input given two days earlier that top Naxal leaders were likely to meet at Bukkadi Bayalu or Kigga forest area of Chikmagalur. Similarly we had alerted all the SPs to be watchful of retaliatory activities by Naxals consequent to the death of Saket Rajan. We had also alerted the Bangalore City Police about the probable protest by Tibetans against the visiting Chinese PM.

I was also aware that as Intelligence officials operate under shadows, whatever good work done by them never comes to public notice. Only their failures are highlighted.

That is the life in Intelligence. Despite all its stresses and strains I must confess that I enjoyed working in the State Intelligence. Working there had given me a better world view. I had met heads of State and governments, Chief Ministers and Governors, captains of industry, and virtually the who's who of society. I had met very powerful and influential people and observed their qualities of greatness as well as pettiness. I was witness to the unfurling of events which would greatly impact society which didn't come easily to any officer. Hence, I considered myself singularly lucky to have worked in State Intelligence.

I must also mention that when Dharam Singh was the CM, we had excellent co-ordination amongst officers who were working closely with the CM. The three secretaries in the CM's secretariat, the OSD and the Media Offticer Dinesh and I shared an excellent rapport. I do admit that working with the CM is a stressful job. The CM's secretary Siddaiah was the stress buster for all of us. He would lighten any serious situation by his timely 'jokes'.

Very soon I got adjusted to my new role as the Chairman and MD of Police Housing Corporation. Even before I could get a proper feel of the job, I was transferred out. I learnt that I had been posted as the Head of Prisons Department. This came as a big shock to me. This was because I had worked for too long outside the police in my career like, Transport, Information and Ecology and Environment and did not want to work in the Prisons Department which was separate from the police. I was already in a non-Police post and I felt that with only five years left for my superannuation, if I continued to work outside the police I might not be considered to be posted as Head of Police Force later when my turn came.

I immediately rushed to Vidhana Soudha to meet the CM, Kumaraswamy. He was in a meeting. When he saw me, he asked me to wait. After a few minutes he called me aside and asked me the purpose of my visit. I told him that I was shocked to know about my sudden transfer. The CM told me that Srikumar, who had been replaced by me was insistent on going back to the Housing Corporation and that his request had been considered. I asked him whether I could not be continued in the same position. He replied in the negative. Seeing the disappointment on my face, he asked me to seek any post I wanted.

Without batting an eyelid, I told him that I would be most happy to work as the Addl DGP in-charge of Recruitment and Training. He instantly asked his Secretary DV Prasad who was present there to get orders issued posting me as Addl DGP, Recruitment and Training. Meanwhile, Kishore Chandra entered the room and CM also told him about my posting. That evening the orders posting me as the Addl DGP of Police Recruitment and Training was issued by the government.

18

My Interactions with Yeddyurappa as CM

I had worked for three years as Additional DGP, Recruitment, and Training, and was to be promoted as DGP in January 2009 consequent to the availability of a vacancy. By that time a lot of political developments had taken place in the State.

After serving as Chief Minister for 20 months, HD Kumaraswamy did not hand over charge to BS Yeddyurappa according to the terms agreed at the time of forming the coalition government. On October 6, 2007 the BJP withdrew its support to the Kumaraswamy government after a fortnight-long political tussle. After HD Kumaraswamy went out of office on October 8, 2007, BS Yeddyurappa became the Chief Minister for the first time on November 12, 2007. But he had to resign a week later on November 19, 2007 as the JD(S) withdrew support to the government. Subsequently, the State came under the President's Rule. Fresh elections were held in May 2008 and the BJP which secured 110 seats, just three short of a majority, formed the government and BS Yeddyurappa became the Chief Minister.

By January 2009, the new government had already completed six months in office. Gopal Hosur, IGP, had replaced Kishore Chandra as the Head of Intelligence. At that time VS Baligar was the Principal Secretary to the CM, and Sudhakar Rao was the Chief Secretary. On January 28, Baligar informed me that the CM had cleared the file regarding my promotion and that I was being posted as DGP, CID.

I had been a little apprehensive about my promotion because of a 'lukewarm' appraisal report given to me by the DG and IGP Sial when I was working as the Addl DGP, Intelligence. Some details are necessary here.

The officer to initiate the ACR of Addl DG Intelligence was the DG and IGP. The reviewing officer was the Chief Secretary and the authority to accept the report was the Chief Minister. When the Chief Minister Dharam Singh was handing over the charge he was expected to write the ACRs of officers directly working under him like the Chief Secretary and his Principal Secretary. But as the CM was only the accepting authority for my appraisal, he could not write his comments about my performance on the ACR format. But I learnt later that he had given a certificate to the Chief Secretary about my performance under him as the Head of Intelligence and asked that it should be included in my Appraisal Report file.

Later when the report for the year 2005-06 was initiated by Sial, I learnt to my shock that he had rated my performance as 'Satisfactory' which could be interpreted that my grading was 'average', the second lowest for any officer. Such a grading, I feared, would adversely affect my chances of promotion to the rank of DGP, especially in the Central Government. While I had not expected to get the highest rating of 'Outstanding' from Sial, I was hopeful of getting a rating of 'Very Good' or at least a rating of 'Good'. However, as the Chief Secretary, the Reviewing Authority, had rated me 'Very Good', my promotion to the rank of DGP in Karnataka was not affected. But I was apprehensive about my empanelment for the post of DGP in the Central Government without which I would not be considered for appointment to posts like heads of Central Armed Police Forces and organisations like CBI and the IB.

Good Track Record

It is not out of place to mention here that ever since I joined the IPS in 1976, I had never been rated less than 'Outstanding' or 'Very Good'. Probably because of my continued good record of service, I faced no problems in getting empanelled to the rank of DGP in Government of India which was announced on March 18, 2010. In hindsight, I realised that my worry was uncalled for.

On getting the call from the Principal Secretary to Yeddyurappa by the end of January 2009, I was pleasantly surprised to hear about my posting as Head of CID as it was one of the most sensitive posts in the Police Department and my posting to that office indicated that the CM had a lot of confidence in me. Very few officers in Karnataka had donned both the posts of Head of Intelligence and Head of CID and I considered myself very lucky.

By January 2011, I was completing two years as Head of CID. Those two years were very hectic as we were entrusted with more and more 'sensitive' cases. I would like to recount a few of such cases here.

Sensational Cases

The first sensitive case we handled was the suicide, in August 2008, of Padmapriya, wife of the then BJP MLA from Udupi Raghupati Bhat. Bhat, who was quite close to the State Home Minister Dr VS Acharya, also from Udupi, had alleged that one of his friends Atul Rao had instigated Padmapriya to leave home and that her suicide in a flat in Delhi was nothing short of murder and that action should be taken against Atul Rao. The case had come to CID after the investigation by the Delhi Police and Udupi police. While the CID could not gather any evidence of murder against the accused, a chargesheet was filed for kidnapping and abetment to suicide. The MLA was not happy with the outcome. I was later told that he had sought the intervention of the Karnataka High Court for re-investigation of this case.

The second case related to the Minister of Food and Civil Supplies Haratalu Halappa, BJP MLA from the Soraba constituency in Shimoga district, the home district of the CM Yeddyurappa. On May 3, 2010, a woman came to the Vinoba

Nagar Police Station in Shimoga town and lodged a 12-page written complaint alleging that the Minister had raped her on the night of November 27, 2009. This issue rocked the entire State and the case was handed over to CID for investigation. *Prima facie,* the complaint had been lodged almost six months after the alleged offence which in itself cast a doubt on the veracity of the complaint. But the lady was in possession of a Compact Disc which had a video recording of the incident. She also had produced a *dhoti* worn by the accused and a petticoat worn by her containing semen stains allegedly belonging to the accused. She explained away the delay in lodging the FIR stating that as the accused had become a Minister, she was apprehensive to lodge a complaint against him. When this matter received wide publicity, the Minister had to resign.

During the course of the investigation, which included a detailed interview with the accused, it was learnt that there existed a relationship between the complainant and the accused and the act was consensual. The former minister also told me that in order to 'finish him politically' certain opposition leaders belonging to his own community had instigated the complainant to lodge the complaint. He claimed that it was a conspiracy to defame him. But as the complainant stuck to her guns, we had no other alternative but to file a chargesheet against Halappa.

Every important functionary of the government asked me the rationale behind the filing of the chargesheet. I took great pains to explain that when the prosecutrix was insisting that an assault on her body, absolving the accused from the case would not be taken well by the courts, public or by the Opposition parties. I told them that as the case had become so sensational if the former minister was not chargesheeted, the government would face tremendous embarrassment. This view of mine came for a lot of criticism.

Halappa faced the trial in the court and he was acquitted of the charge.

The next case related to the allegation of rape, unnatural sex and cheating against 'godman' Swami Nityananda of Bidadi Ashram. Since the trial of this case has recently begun, I would not like to comment about its investigation by CID. Suffice it to say that a large number of 'bigwigs' were very unhappy with CID in general and me in particular for prosecuting the Swamiji.

The fourth case related to the export of iron ore from the Belekeri Port in Uttara Kannada district. In June 2010, the Asst Conservator of Forests, Ankola gave a report in the local police station that his department had registered a case under the Forest Act and had seized about five hundred thousand metric tonnes of iron ore which had been kept in Belekeri port for export. He added that certain mining companies in connivance with the authorities had succeeded in transporting the seized ore. On the directions by the DG and IGP of Karnataka State, the CID took up this case for investigation.

Fifteen teams were constituted to conduct the investigation. The entire investigation was done under the direct supervision of Charan Reddy, DIG. Twelve different companies who were involved in the transport of the ore were in the list of the accused. The CM held several review meetings and gave us directions that we should not spare any accused. As the investigation to be done was very vast, we had to dedicate a very large portion of our resources to the investigation of these cases. Despite all our efforts, the investigation proceeded at a slow pace as we had to examine voluminous documents.

In the last week of August 2010, while dealing with a petition concerning this case, a High Court Judge had made a passing remark about the slow pace of investigation of the 'Belekeri Case' and handing over the case to the CBI for further investigation. The Judge had also summoned me to appear before the court and submit a status report on the investigation done so far.

The remarks by the Judge were communicated to the Home Minister by the Prosecutor concerned. The Home

Minister held a meeting to discuss the case. On August 31, a meeting took place and surprisingly the CM also attended the same. During the meeting, it was felt that the High Court might hand over the investigation of the case to the CBI and if that was done, the CBI which functioned under the Central Government ruled by the UPA would "try to settle political scores". The consensus was that we should submit the chargesheet in the case at the earliest.

On September 2, I appeared before the High Court and explained about the progress of the investigation and assured the court that the final reports would be placed as early as possible. The first chargesheet in the case was filed in December 2010.

Though we had filed chargesheets against many important companies and individuals, some persons had commented that the CID hadn't unearthed the origin of the ore and cause investigation against the mine owners. The CID was investigating only the matter related to the theft of the seized ore from the port premises. Hence our officers had opined that we should not go beyond our mandate as it would be very time consuming and we didn't have any resources like the CBI to spread the net wide. Moreover, regarding the source of the seized ore, the Forest Department had already registered a case and was investigating. Besides, we were under pressure to complete the investigation early.

Attack on Churches

Another sensitive matter was the investigation of 'Church Blast' cases. In 2008, over 30 cases of minor blasts, arson, mischief and desecration in churches in Dakshina Kannada, Udupi, Chikmagalur and Bangalore districts had been reported. The Centre had taken these incidents seriously and had issued a notice to the State Government under Article 355 of the Constitution. The then leader of Bajrang Dal Mahendra Kumar had claimed before the media that it was his organization which had been responsible for the attacks on churches and prayer halls. He had stated that incidents of forced conversion had prompted such attacks. He had retracted his statement later.

Investigation of a few such cases had been given to the CID. In connection with the investigation of one of these cases, I had been called to attend a meeting held by the Chief Minister Yeddyurappa at the National Institute of Advanced Studies Guest House in Bangalore. The CM expressed his unhappiness that we had not yet nabbed any culprits. He stated that he had been told that a certain leader of a political party was behind the attack in Bangalore with the intention of bringing a bad name to his government. I told him that we didn't have any such evidence so far but would definitely look into that aspect. Further investigation did not throw any evidence about instigation by any opposition party leaders in the case.

Another case which had raised national interest was based on a *Habeas Corpus* petition filed in the Karnataka High Court about the kidnapping of a Hindu girl by name Silja Raj of Chamarajanagar district by a taxi driver Asghar of Kerala. The High Court had wanted us to investigate whether there was a practice called 'Love Jihad' where Hindu girls would be enticed and converted to Islam. We filed a report that most such cases were love affairs and were not attributable to any organizations. I was informed by many that this view of the CID was not taken well by the powers that be.

On January 31, 2011, Dr Ajai Kumar Singh, DG and IGP of Karnataka State was slated to superannuate. At that time, apart from him, three officers of the DGP rank were functioning in Karnataka. The seniormost of the three was Jija Harisingh, a lady officer of 1975 batch who was the DGP Home Guards and Fire Force. The next in line was Sharat Saxena of my batch (1976) who was working as DGP and CMD, Police Housing Corporation. I was the third in line. ST Ramesh, also of my batch, who was the DGP Training, was the fourth.

The Supreme Court had mandated, in the Prakash Singh case of police reforms that, the DGP (HoPF) of a State had to be selected from amongst the three seniormost officers who are in the scale of DGP and those who were empanelled for promotion by the UPSC.

As Jija Harisingh and Saxena were retiring from service along with Dr Ajai Kumar Singh on January 31, 2011, the government had to choose only either Ramesh or me as the next DG and IGP. (In Karnataka the HoPF is designated as DG and IGP and is the highest post in the Police Department.) Though we both belonged to the same batch and had the same number of years of service in the IPS, in the *inter se* seniority of the 1976 batch of IPS, I was senior to him. Hence by November 2010, there was wide speculation that I would succeed Dr Ajai Kumar Singh as the next DG and IGP of the State.

On December 20, I got information from very reliable sources that the matter of the selection of the DG and IGP had been discussed and that the Chief Minister had indicated that I would be selected as the next DG and IGP.

Supreme Court Order Not Followed

The very next day, on December 21, Shankar Bidari, an IPS officer of 1978 batch, then working in the rank of Addl DGP, gave a representation to the government that for selecting the next DG and IGP, all those officers who have put in 30 years of service in the IPS should be considered and not just the two officers who are of the DGP rank. He also sent a similar representation to the Union Public Service Commission (UPSC). I immediately sensed that something was going wrong.

The UPSC, probably acting on Bidari's representation, wrote a letter to the Karnataka Government on January 20, 2011, to send the dossiers of all IPS officers who had completed 30 years of service. The letter was received by the State Government only ten days before the retirement of Dr Ajai Kumar Singh. I took objection to this move by the UPSC on the ground that the letter was violative of the orders of the Supreme Court. Hence I filed a petition in the Central

Administrative Tribunal and got a stay against the operation of the letter.

The Government of Karnataka was now in a dilemma. The only option available to it was to make interim arrangements to fill up the post of DG and IGP when it became vacant on the evening of January 31. The time-tested administrative practice was to appoint the seniormost officer to any post on an interim basis. I was pretty sure that I would be made the in-Charge DG and IGP as I was the seniormost officer.

On the evening of January 31, I came to know that when the Chief Secretary had put up the file recommending my name for holding a concurrent charge as the State DG and IGP, the Chief Minister Yeddyurappa, overruled the noting and ordered that ST Ramesh should hold the concurrent charge.

Both Ramesh and I were left with seven more months of service. Both of us were slated to retire on July 31, 2011.

My petition in the Administrative Tribunal was still pending. I had decided to take the matter to its logical end. On April 21, 2011, the Tribunal upheld my contention and ordered the UPSC to prepare a panel of officers eligible for the post of DG and IGP based on the directions of the Supreme Court.

On May 14, the UPSC held the meeting for empanelling officers to the post of DG and IGP, Karnataka. The State Government had sent the names of four officers, who were at the relevant time holding the rank of DGP. Apart from me, the names of ST Ramesh, N Achuta Rao, and MK Srivastava were on the list. The UPSC empanelled only three officers and left out the name of Ramesh. I was ranked first on the list. I was, therefore, certain that I would be posted as the next DG and IGP.

Aggrieved by the action of the UPSC in not empanelling him, Ramesh, who was also to retire the same day along with me, approached the Central Administrative Tribunal to direct the UPSC to include his name in the panel for appointment to the post of DG and IGP. The Tribunal ordered the State of Karnataka not to make the appointment of DG and IGP till the disposal of Ramesh's petition. I impleaded myself as one of the parties. On June 17th, the CAT rejected the application of Ramesh.

Meanwhile, Ramesh gave another petition to the UPSC, through the State Government, that injustice had been caused to him.

With only 44 days left for my retirement, I was hopeful that I would, at last, become the DG and IGP of Karnataka State.

The State Government did not take any action to appoint a regular DG and IGP and I was told that it was dilly-dallying over the matter because, if I were to be appointed DG and IGP, as per the Supreme Court directions in the Prakash Singh's case, I might have to be given tenure of two years.

Many senior officers told me that the government was biding for time and would not take any action till I retired from service. I was told that the government appeared happy with in-charge arrangements in place for the post of DG and IGP. (Karnataka was following the pattern of Gujarat where no regular DGP had been appointed for a considerable length of time. Tamil Nadu also was happy with such an arrangement. It was only in 2018 that the Supreme Court frowned upon in-charge arrangements and directed the States to appoint DGP on a regular basis.) As it became very clear to me that I would miss the bus, I wanted to fight till the very end.

On June 27, I gave a letter to the State Government that as it had not acted on the orders of the Central Administrative Tribunal, I intended to take up a contempt petition against the Chief Secretary. The government remained unmoved.

On July 1, which happened to be a Friday, I went to the official residence of the CM BS Yeddyurappa, to make a personal representation. He had gone for a walk and I was waiting in the visitors' room. At 8.30 AM, he returned home along with his son Vijayendra. On seeing me the CM came to the visitors room. I wished him and told him that I had only 29 days left to retire. He said, "I know you are a good officer, we will do something." I told him that time was running out. He said, "Let Ramesh continue as in-Charge DGP. I will give you a good job after your retirement with a monthly salary of ₹1.5 lakh with a car, driver, secretary, etc."

I told the CM that it was the desire of every IPS officer to head the police department at least for a day and I was not an exception. I was placed on the top of the panel sent by UPSC and deserved the post. I told him that if I were appointed the DG and IGP, I would gracefully retire at the end of the month. I also told him that I didn't want any sinecures after my retirement.

Yeddyurappa said, "Okay, I will see what I can do. I have high regards for you," and started getting up from his chair. I told him to kindly consider my genuine request. He said, "Let me see," and concluded the meeting.

I was then certain that I would not be posted as the DG and IGP. From the residence of the Chief Minister, I drove down to the residence of the Chief Secretary SV Ranganath and told him about my meeting with the CM a few minutes earlier. I informed him that I would be filing a contempt petition in the Administrative Tribunal against him the same day. He told me to wait till July 4, which was a Monday, so that he could speak to the CM and let me know.

On July 2 the Chief Secretary told me that the matter had been discussed at a very high-level meeting and an opinion emerged that as the petition to the UPSC by Ramesh was still pending, it would not amount to contempt of court if the next DG and IGP was not appointed by the State Government immediately.

Won the Battle to Lose the War

On Monday, July 4, I filed my petition in the Central Administrative Tribunal against the Karnataka Government for contempt of court. On that day, as my lawyer had not come to the court, I decided to argue the matter myself. As the court convened, I moved my matter explaining the urgency. The matter was listed for hearing the same day and notice was issued to the government pleader. When the matter was taken up for hearing at 12.45 PM, I was surprised to see the State Advocate General Ashok Harnahalli, appear for the government. Everyone in the court hall was surprised seeing him. Probably it was the rarest of the rare occasions when the Advocate General was making an appearance in the Central Administrative Tribunal.

Before I started my argument I remarked that while I had no degree in law and absolutely inexperienced in court matters, the State had sent its top Legal Officer to fight me. I quoted a Kannada proverb and said that it is like using a *brahmastra* against a sparrow. I argued for 45 minutes and convinced the Tribunal to issue the notice of contempt of court to the State Government. At 3.30 PM, I collected the notice from the court, went to Vidhana Soudha and served it on the Chief Secretary. I was told by the legal fraternity that I had created a record of sorts.

The choice before the government was limited. In the panel sent by the UPSC, there were only three names. Of the three, Srivastava had by then retired from service. The government had to appoint either me or Achuta Rao. The very next day, the government appointed Neelam Achuta Rao as the DG and IGP. The reason given for overlooking my name was that I had only three weeks of service left, whereas Rao had four and a half months. I had won the battle but lost the war.

Even to this day, I have not understood why the CM Yeddyurappa was so adamant in not appointing me as the DG and IGP. When he had indicated that I would be made the next DG and IGP on December 20, 2010 what made him change his mind within 41 days is still a mystery to me.

One theory that was making the rounds at that time was that someone very close to the CM had told him that as

I had worked as Head of Intelligence with the Congress government, I was loyal to the Congress party and would not help the BJP. Another theory was that I was projected as a no-nonsense officer (which I was) and would not obey any improper, illegal or unreasonable orders. My work as the Head of the CID is said to have been quoted as an example. What I am definitely certain is that a section of Police officers, who had feared that if I became the DG and IGP, I would go to court and get two years extended tenure, and thereby spoil their chances of promotion, prevented my promotion to the coveted post.

The tabloid *Bangalore Mirror* in its issue dated August 19, 2011, mentioned that Swami Nityananda reportedly told his advocate CV Nagesh that it was because of his curse that I was denied the post of DG and IGP.

I do not know what the truth is.

Index